**ATTP 3-34.80** (FM 3-34.230, FM 5-33, and TC 5-230)
July 2010

I0026814

# GEOSPATIAL ENGINEERING

DISTRIBUTION RESTRICTION: Approved for public release; distribution is unlimited.

# HEADQUARTERS, DEPARTMENT OF THE ARMY

**Published by Books Express Publishing**
**Books Express Publishing, 2011**
**ISBN 978-1-78039-980-5**

**Books Express publications are available from all good retail and online booksellers. For publishing proposals and direct ordering please contact us at: info@books-express.com**

**\*ATTP 3-34.80 (FM 3-34.230, FM 5-33, and TC 5-230)**

ARMY TACTICS, TECHNIQUES, AND PROCEDURES
NO. 3-34.80 (FM 3-34.230, FM 5-33, and TC 5-230)

HEADQUARTERS
DEPARTMENT OF THE ARMY
Washington, DC 29 July 2010

# Geospatial Engineering

## Contents

Page

---

**Distribution Restriction:** Approved for public release; distribution is unlimited.

\*This publication will supersede FM 3-34.230, 3 August 2000; FM 5-33, 11 July 1990; and Training Circular 5-230, 28 November 2003.

# Figures

# Tables

This page intentionally left blank.

# Preface

Geospatial engineering capabilities have experienced significant improvements due to organizational changes, technological advancements, and emerging best practices. Geospatial engineering leverages ever-finer temporal and spatial resolutions from additional sensors and platforms that allow increased volumes and more complex data. New methods and technologies provide additional utility and the ability to work effectively within a broad pool of partners and allies.

Army Tactics, Techniques, and Procedures (ATTP) 3-34.80 describes doctrine for geospatial engineering operations at all echelons. It is an extension of Field Manual (FM) 3-34 and is linked to joint and other Army doctrine to ensure its usefulness for operational-level commanders and staff. This manual serves as a guide for the integration of geospatial engineering in support of full spectrum operations at all echelons, with added focus on describing the "how-to" within divisions and the brigades. This publication applies to the Active Army, Army National Guard, Army National Guard of the United States, and the United States Army Reserve unless otherwise stated.

ATTP 3-34.80 combines, updates, and supersedes material from FM 3-34.230, FM 5-33, and Training Circular (TC) 5-230 and is built directly on new or revised joint and Army doctrine, notably Army capstone doctrine found in FM 3-0 and engineer keystone doctrine presented in FM 3-34. This revision also captures the results of lessons learned and observations from recent operational experiences in Afghanistan, Iraq, and other locations, to include the challenges of operating in complex terrain. Other changes that have directly affected this manual include—

- Creation of geospatial planning cells (GPCs).
- Effects of Army modularity on the topographic engineer companies.
- Replacement of the battlefield operating systems with the warfighting functions.
- Placement of organic geospatial engineering teams within the modular support and functional brigades and the brigade combat teams (BCTs).
- Replacement of the engineer battlefield assessment with the engineer's running estimate.
- Elimination of the term *battlespace* and the subsequent change from *engineer battlespace functions* to simply the *engineer functions* of combat, general, and geospatial engineering.
- Evolution of the concept of geospatial intelligence (GEOINT), consisting of imagery, imagery intelligence (IMINT), and geospatial information (GI).
- Revision of the joint definition for geospatial engineering.

This manual will serve as a reference document for engineer commanders and staff, leaders, training developers, and doctrine developers throughout the Army. It will be a primary manual for instructional purposes in the United States Army Engineer School (USAES) and will help other Army branch schools in teaching the integration of geospatial engineering capabilities into Army operations.

The manual is organized into three chapters, with supporting appendixes, which sequentially describe geospatial engineering, the roles and responsibilities for integrating geospatial support at the various echelons, and how it is integrated within the Army's operations process. A brief description of each of the chapters and appendixes is provided below.

- Chapter 1 describes the role of geospatial engineering in supporting full spectrum operations and its importance for understanding the operational environment (OE).
- Chapter 2 discusses the geospatial engineering capabilities that reside within each of the echelons down to the BCT. It also describes the critical roles and responsibilities that national- and defense-level agencies and Army units and staffs have in providing geospatial engineering in support of Army operations.
- Chapter 3 focuses on the "how-to" for integrating geospatial engineering capabilities into the Army operations process.

- Appendix A provides examples of geospatial products that aid terrain visualization and support decisionmaking.
- Appendix B provides information on gathering, storing, and disseminating relevant digital terrain data that support operations and enable decisionmaking.
- Appendix C outlines the format and provides examples of GI for inclusion in Army mission plans and orders.
- Appendix D describes the six characteristics of terrain that geospatial engineers analyze in determining the terrain's effects on operations.
- Appendix E further describes the geospatial engineering organizations that support each echelon down to BCT.
- Appendix F describes the digital topographic support system (DTSS) family of systems that geospatial engineers use to support mission requirements.

Terms that have joint or Army definitions are identified in the text. Glossary references: The glossary lists all proponent terms for ATTP 3-34.80. Text references: Definitions printed in boldface in the text indicate that this manual is the proponent manual. These terms and their definitions will be incorporated into the next revision of FM 1-02. For other definitions in the text, the term is italicized, and the number of the proponent manual follows the definition.

The proponent for this publication is the United States Army Training and Doctrine Command (TRADOC). Send comments and recommendations on Department of the Army (DA) Form 2028 (Recommended Changes to Publications and Blank Forms) directly to Commandant, USAES, ATTN: ATZT-TDD-E, 320 MANSCEN Loop, Suite 270, Fort Leonard Wood, Missouri 65473-8929. Submit an electronic DA Form 2028 or comments and recommendations in the DA Form 2028 format by e-mail to <leon.mdottddengdoc@conus.army.mil>.

Unless stated otherwise, masculine nouns or pronouns do not refer exclusively to men.

# Introduction

The three engineer functions are combat, general, and geospatial engineering. Geospatial engineering is both an art and a science that pertains to the generation, management, analysis, and dissemination of positionally accurate GI that is tied to some portion of the earth's surface. These actions provide mission-tailored data, tactical decision aids (TDAs), and visualization products that enable the commander and staff to visualize the OE. Geospatial engineering plays a major role in engineer reconnaissance (see FM 3-34.170) and the integrated support of combat and general engineering.

GI that is timely, accurate, and relevant is a critical enabler throughout the operations process. Geospatial engineers, engineer coordinators (ENCOORDs), and other staff members help in the analysis of the meaning of activities and significantly contribute to anticipating, estimating, and warning of possible future events. They provide the foundation for developing shared situational awareness, improve understanding of capabilities and limitations for friendly forces (as well as the adversary), and highlight other conditions of the OE.

In addition to mastering their respective areas of expertise, geospatial engineers, ENCOORDs, and other staff members must possess a thorough understanding of tactics and the application of combat power to be able to tailor GI to support the commander's visualization and, ultimately, decisionmaking. New methods and technologies provide additional utility and the ability to work effectively within a broad pool of partners and allies. Advancements in technology and the ready access to an abundance of information can easily lead to information overload. Planners must be able to analyze the situation through the mission and operational variables, grasp the military significance of the challenges and opportunities presented, and manage information to enable situational understanding and ultimately support decisionmaking.

This manual describes the application of geospatial engineering in support of Army forces conducting full spectrum operations within the framework of joint operations and the roles and responsibilities of geospatial engineers, ENCOORDs, and other staff members. It also acknowledges that Army doctrine remains dynamic—balancing current capabilities and situations with projected requirements for future operations. As geospatial engineering capabilities continue to improve through organizational changes, technology advancements, and emerging best practices, leaders and planners at all levels will be charged to leverage those improvements and adapt the processes and procedures described in this manual to meet demands and provide the most effective geospatial support possible to the commander.

**This page intentionally left blank**.

# Chapter 1

# Geospatial Engineering in Support of Full Spectrum Operations

In full spectrum operations, Army forces adapt to the requirements of the OE. A critical aspect of applying combat power and successfully conducting operations rests on the collective ability of commanders and staffs to see and comprehend the OE. This chapter describes geospatial engineering and its role in enabling commanders and staffs to better understand the OE through terrain analysis and terrain visualization of the physical environment.

## OVERVIEW

1-1. *Geospatial information and services* (GI&S) is the collection, information extraction, storage, dissemination, and exploitation of geodetic, geomagnetic, imagery (both commercial and national source), gravimetric, aeronautical, topographic, hydrographic, littoral, cultural, and toponymic data accurately referenced to a precise location on the earth's surface. Geospatial services include tools that enable users to access and manipulate data, and they also include instruction, training, laboratory support, and guidance for the use of geospatial data (Joint Publication [JP] 2-03). The availability of commercial off-the-shelf geospatial data software applications enables a wide variety of military and civilian users to apply GI&S to an assortment of situations. Common military applications of GI&S include support to planning, training, and operations—including navigation, mission planning, mission rehearsal, modeling, simulation, and precise targeting. Automated geospatial applications can enhance map features (such as elevation) that may not be discernable on a map to enable more detailed analysis. Within the Army, GI&S is tactically employed by geospatial engineers to better understand the physical environment; to provide the geospatial foundation for developing shared situational awareness; and to improve the understanding of friendly forces, capabilities, the adversary, and other conditions of the OE—this is geospatial engineering.

### GEOSPATIAL ENGINEERING

1-2. Geospatial engineering, along with combat and general engineering, comprise the engineer functions. These categories of related engineer capabilities and activities are grouped together to help joint force commanders integrate, synchronize, and direct engineer operations. FM 3-34 provides more information on the engineer functions and its role in support of full spectrum operations. *Geospatial engineering* is the art and science of applying geographic information to enable understanding of the physical environment for military operations. The art is the ability to understand mission, enemy, terrain and weather, troops and support available, time available, civil considerations (METT-TC) and the GI available—including intent of use and limitations—to explain the military significance of the terrain to the commander and staff, and create geospatial products for decisionmaking; the science is the ability to exploit GI, producing spatially accurate products for measurement, mapping, visualization, modeling, and all types of analysis of the terrain (FM 3-34).

1-3. To enable understanding of the physical environment, geospatial engineers perform the following four major functions:

- Generate, acquire, extract, and fuse timely, relevant, and accurate high-resolution GI to provide the appropriate data sets to the Army Battle Command System (ABCS).
- Analyze data, aided by computer algorithms and terrain reasoning tools, to enable prediction and provide actionable information for decisionmaking.

● Manage, warehouse, and validate the geospatial foundation of the common operational picture (COP) in a standardized, configurable, interoperable format to support training, simulations, and operations.

● Disseminate geospatial data updates to and from ABCS to maintain a COP and distribute GI to the appropriate level to facilitate operations.

1-4.   These four major functions (see figure 1-1) are performed by both organic and augmenting geospatial engineer elements at the theater, corps, division, and brigade levels. The roles and responsibilities for performing geospatial engineering within each of the echelons are further discussed in chapter 2.

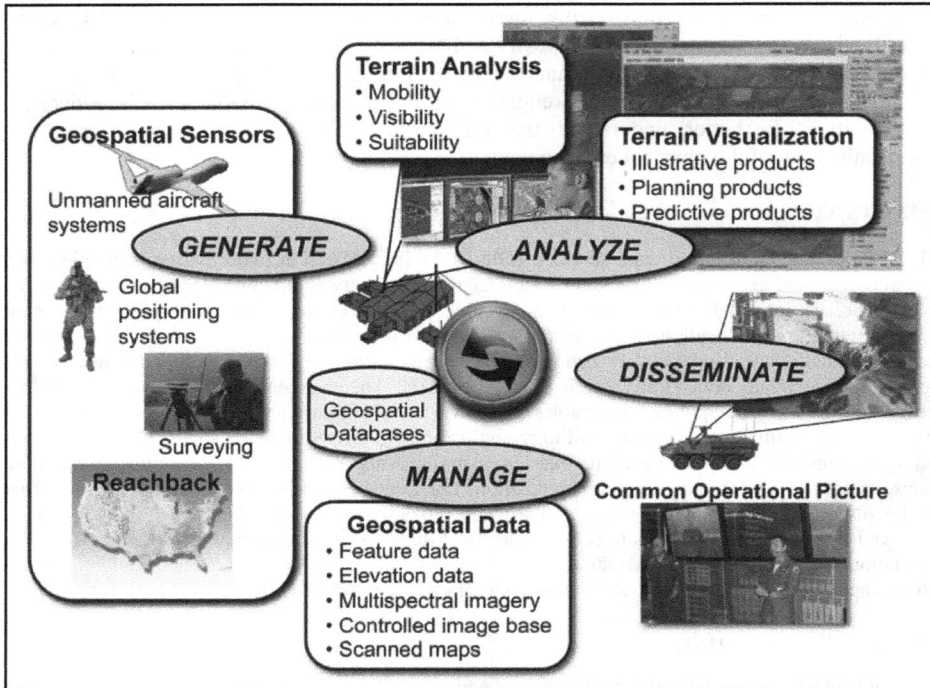

**Figure 1-1. The four major functions of geospatial engineering**

## Geospatial Information

1-5.   The Army defines **geospatial information as the foundation information on which all other information about the physical environment is referenced to form the common operational picture**. GI provides the basic framework for visualizing the OE. It is information produced by multiple sources to common interoperable data standards. It may be presented in the form of printed maps, charts, digital files, and publications; in digital simulation and modeling databases; in photographic form; or in the form of digitized maps and charts. Its effectiveness as an enabler is directly proportional to its currency, accuracy, and relevance. Joint doctrine defines *geospatial information* as the information that identifies the geographic location and characteristics of natural or constructed features and boundaries on the earth, including statistical data and information derived from—among other things—remote sensing, mapping, and surveying technologies and mapping, charting, geodetic data and related products (JP 2-03).

### Geospatial Data

1-6.   Gathering geospatial data from multiple sources and making them readily available to multiple entities enables the foundation of the COP (geospatial data management is discussed in appendix B).

Geospatial data may include information such as scanned digital map displays, elevation data, imagery, and feature data.

1-7. Compressed arc digitized raster graphics (CADRGs) are scanned digital map displays of unclassified maps and charts and are available by stock number from the Defense Logistics Agency (DLA) on compact disc (CD) or can be downloaded from National Geospatial-Intelligence Agency (NGA) websites. All CADRG data use the world geodetic system-84 datum, regardless of the datum used in the creation of the original map or chart. The data are published in NGA's raster product format, which can be read by the ABCS that incorporates the commercial joint mapping tool kit and other GI&S programs such as Falcon View™. CADRGs consist of paper maps of all scales that have been scanned and are suitable for digital map backgrounds. CADRGs at 1:50,000 and 1:100,000 scale are the most widely used for tactical operations. City maps at a 1:12,500 scale or better are also available, but will not show all buildings; however, this can be achieved using georeferenced imagery. Like imagery, CADRG digital maps do not provide more detail when viewed at a higher resolution (zoomed-in)—this just makes the existing features appear larger. The positional accuracy of CADRG is no better than the accuracy of the source map or chart (±50 meters horizontal accuracy for 1:50,000 scale topographic line maps [TLMs] and ±100 meters for 1:100,000).

1-8. Elevation data have varying levels of detail: Digital Terrain Elevation Data (DTED®) Level 1 (roughly 90-meter post spacing, bare earth), DTED Level 2 (30-meter post spacing, bare earth), shuttle radar topography mission 2 (30-meter post spacing, reflective surface or "treetop" data), and high-resolution elevation data. DTED is intended for lower-resolution viewing of large areas and is not appropriate for tactical planning that requires higher-resolution viewing. DTED Level 1 provides approximately the same level of detail that the contour lines of a 1:250,000-scale map joint operational graphic does. Maps at a 1:50,000 scale can be used successfully with DTED Level 2 and shuttle radar topography mission elevation data for line-of-sight (LOS) analyses and weapons fans, but the use of DTED Level 1 with 1:50,000-scale CADRGs should be discouraged due to inaccuracies in lower-resolution elevation data. DTED 1 and 2 data can be ordered through DLA on CD or downloaded from NGA Web sites. Most government and commercial software applications that read raster product format will also read DTED data. Light detection and ranging (LIDAR) is a remote sensing technology that measures properties of scattered light to find elevation data. This technology is useful in deriving 1-meter gridded bare earth digital elevation model (DEM) (32-bit geographic tagged image file format), and three-dimensional (3-D) feature extraction for urban areas and vegetation (shape files).

1-9. Georeferenced imagery typically consists of Controlled Image Base® (CIB) 5 (5-meter resolution), CIB 1 (1-meter resolution), and commercial satellite imagery. CIB imagery is useful for image map backgrounds and to display features that are not represented on digital map backgrounds. However, the image map is not a replacement for standard TLMs. CIB 1 can be used for urban areas, but may not provide the desired detailed resolution needed for urban analysis. In this situation, higher-resolution imagery from commercial or national sources is better suited.

1-10. Feature data, also referred to as vector data, provide digital representations of man-made or natural objects as points, lines, or polygons (such as wells, roads, and forests). Each feature can include embedded information (attribution), such as bank heights for bodies of water, type of road surface, road width, and bridge load-bearing classification, which can be accessed by "right-clicking" the mouse pointer while holding it over the feature. Fully attributed feature data can be used to perform automated terrain analysis.

*Terrain Analysis*

1-11. Terrain and weather are natural conditions that profoundly influence operations. They are both neutral and favor neither side unless one side is more familiar with, or better prepared to operate in, the resulting conditions. Terrain includes natural features (such as rivers and mountains) and man-made features (such as cities, airfields, and bridges). Terrain directly affects the selection of objectives and the location, movement, and control of forces. It also influences protective measures and the effectiveness of both lethal and nonlethal weapons and other systems. Effective use of terrain reduces the effects of enemy fires, increases the effects of friendly fires, and facilitates surprise.

1-12. Weather affects all operations. In contrast to climate, which is the prevailing pattern of temperature, wind velocity, and precipitation in a specific area measured over a period of years, weather describes the conditions of temperature, wind velocity, precipitation, and visibility at a specific place and time. Climate is typically used in strategic and operational planning that covers a large geographically diverse area, whereas weather is more applicable to tactical planning where its effect on operations is limited in scale and duration. Both climate and weather present opportunities and challenges in every operation. They affect the conditions of the physical environment and the capabilities and performance of Soldiers, equipment, and weapon systems. Table 1-1 shows some of the weather conditions to be considered when analyzing the terrain.

**Table 1-1. Weather effects considerations within terrain analysis**

| Weather Condition | Considerations when performing terrain analysis |
|---|---|
| Temperature | • Freezing temperatures can amplify the effects of precipitation on man-made structures (such as roads and bridges) and affect trafficability.<br>• Extremely high temperatures affect contrasting in thermal imagery. |
| Humidity | • Humidity can affect materials (such as soil and concrete) used in constructing airfields, roads, and combat trails. |
| Precipitation | • Rain and snowfall affect trafficability on and off roads.<br>• Heavy rainfall can render low-lying areas unusable. |
| Visibility | • Dust, fog, day/night conditions affect the effective distances used in line-of-sight analysis and displays. |
| High winds (> 35 knots) | • High winds reduce visibility by blowing sand, dust, and other battlefield debris, which can affect movement rates.<br>• Wind can improve trafficability by causing soil to dry faster.<br>• Wind can amplify the effects of temperatures below 40 degrees Fahrenheit (wind chill). |
| Cloud cover | • Reduced ceilings impact the line of sight of friendly and enemy aerial attack and reconnaissance platforms.<br>• Cloud cover impairs aerial and satellite imagery. |

1-13. *Terrain analysis* **is the study of the terrain's properties and how they change over time, with use, and under varying weather conditions. Terrain analysis starts with the collection, verification, processing, revision, and construction of source data. It requires the analysis of climatology (current and forecasted weather conditions), natural and man-made features, and enemy or friendly vehicle performance metrics. Terrain analysis is a technical process and requires the expertise of geospatial information technicians and geospatial engineers.** Terrain analysis evaluates the characteristics of natural and man-made terrain that are grouped within the following six areas, which are discussed in appendix D:

- Hydrology.
- Surface configuration.
- Soil composition.
- Vegetation.
- Obstacles.
- Man-made features.

1-14. For tactical operations, terrain is analyzed using the five military aspects of terrain expressed in the memory aid OAKOC: **O**bservation and fields of fire, **A**venues of approach, **K**ey and decisive terrain, **O**bstacles, **C**over and concealment. Table 1-2 shows terrain analysis considerations in relation to military aspects of terrain. The effectiveness of terrain analysis in support of mission planning and operational requirements is directly proportional to the availability of current, accurate geospatial data. This desired condition depends on the effective generation and management of geospatial data at every echelon from combatant command to deployed BCT. Geospatial data management is discussed further in appendix B.

**Table 1-2. Terrain analysis considerations within OAKOC**

| Military Aspects of Terrain | Terrain Analysis Considerations |
|---|---|
| Observation and fields of fire | • Analyze terrain factors that impact observation capabilities for electronic and LOS surveillance systems, and unaided visual observation.<br>• Determine terrain effects on the trajectory of munitions (direct and indirect fire) and tube elevation.<br>• Evaluate potential EAs based on—<br>  ▪ Defensibility of the area (for friendly as well as enemy forces) based on terrain impacts on specific equipment or equipment positions.<br>  ▪ Vulnerability of friendly forces based on enemy observation and fields of fire. |
| Avenue of approach | • Identify mobility corridors based on equipment and preferred doctrinal formations.<br>• Categorize mobility corridors by size or type of force that they can accommodate.<br>• Evaluate AAs by comparing mobility (such as speed based on vegetation, slope, obstacles, and soil conditions), observation, sustainability, and accessibility. |
| Key terrain | • Display nominations for key terrain based on the mission, concept of the operation, threat, and environment.<br>• Consider the following key terrain based on the environment:<br>  ▪ Urban environment: tall structures, choke points, intersections, bridges, and industrial complexes.<br>  ▪ Open environment: terrain features that dominate an area with good observations and fields of fire, choke points, and bridges. |
| Obstacles | • Evaluate the effects of natural and man-made obstacles based on—<br>  ▪ Current and projected weather conditions.<br>  ▪ Type of movement (foot, wheeled, tracked, or air).<br>  ▪ Capabilities of vehicles and equipment.<br>• Analyze water features (as well as surface drainage) to include width, depth, velocity, and bank slope for potential river-(or other gap-) crossing sites.<br>• Identify and evaluate impacts of potential dam breaches.<br>• Analyze on- and off-road surface conditions based on—<br>  ▪ Slope.<br>  ▪ Vegetation.<br>  ▪ Complex terrain.<br>  ▪ Road characteristics (curves, slope, width, clearance, and load-bearing [bridge classification]).<br>• Analyze air movement obstructions including—<br>  ▪ Elevation that exceeds aircraft service ceilings.<br>  ▪ Restrictions to flying nap of the earth or vertical obstructions that impact flight profiles (such as buildings, power lines, and communication towers).<br>• Create the CCM to reflect severely restricted, restricted, and unrestricted terrain on the COO and MCOO. |
| Cover and concealment | • Analyze aspects of the terrain that offer protection from bullets, exploding rounds, and explosive hazards (cover).<br>• Analyze aspects of the terrain that offer protection from observation (from aerial and ground detection), such as vegetation and surface configuration (concealment). |

Legend:
| | | | |
|---|---|---|---|
| AA | avenue of approach | LOS | line of sight |
| CCM | cross-country mobility | MCOO | modified combined obstacle overlay |
| COO | combined obstacle overlay | OAKOC | observation and fields of fire, avenues of approach, key terrain, obstacles, and cover and concealment |
| EA | engagement area | | |

## Terrain Visualization

1-15. While terrain analysis is more of a science, terrain visualization is an art. It is a fundamental leadership skill and involves seeing the terrain and understanding its impact on the situation, including its effects on both friendly and enemy capabilities. It is the identification and understanding of terrain aspects that can be exploited to gain advantage over the enemy as well as those most likely to be used by the enemy. It is the subjective evaluation of the terrain's physical attributes as well as the performance capabilities of vehicles, equipment, and personnel that must cross over and occupy the terrain.

1-16. Engineers at every echelon are considered terrain-visualization experts. As such, they visually present terrain-related relevant information (RI) to commanders and staffs to help them conceptualize important aspects of the physical environment and support decisionmaking. To do so, they first must be able to identify challenges to the commander's ability to move and maneuver, protect the force, and sustain the operation. Likewise, they must also look for opportunities to directly impact adversaries' freedom of action.

1-17. Advanced technology provides the capability to use and combine geospatial data in different ways to create interactive and dynamic, customized visual products. For example, terrain reasoning products can integrate enemy and other man-made obstacles with natural restrictions of the terrain to help determine and show the best avenues of approach (AAs) toward a given objective. Additionally, geospatial products can now leverage a wider variety of data, including those from other intelligence sources (such as signals intelligence [SIGINT] and human intelligence [HUMINT]) through collaborative processes, to provide more accurate, comprehensive, and relevant products. A good example of this is the ability to add more dimensions to standard geospatial products. The third dimension provides the capability to visualize in-depth, while the fourth dimension integrates the elements of time and movement.

1-18. ENCOORDs must work with geospatial engineers to fully help others in seeing the terrain more effectively. Geospatial engineers evaluate the available geospatial content for suitability in performing analysis and in providing needed visualization products. They apply filters to screen irrelevant content that could slow analysis or clutter displays. They also check the integrity of content to ensure its completeness and logical consistency and then perform analysis to generate TDAs. Terrain visualization products contain standardized symbols and colors to ensure quality and understandability. Whenever possible, operational graphics should be included in visualization products to provide a point of reference. This is especially useful when products are used to update a maneuver commander.

## SUPPORTING GEOSPATIAL INTELLIGENCE

1-19. *Geospatial intelligence* is the exploitation and analysis of imagery and geospatial information to describe, assess, and visually depict physical features and geographically referenced activities on the earth. Geospatial intelligence consists of imagery, imagery intelligence, and geospatial information (JP 2-03). The GEOINT enterprise encompasses all activities involved in the planning, collecting, processing, analyzing, exploiting, and disseminating of spatial information to gain intelligence about the OE; visually depicting this knowledge; and fusing the acquired knowledge with other information through analysis and visualization processes. GEOINT products help in describing the OE's effects on enemy and friendly capabilities and broad courses of action (COAs). The use of GEOINT can be categorized in the following five general areas (see JP 2-03 for more information):

- General military intelligence (MI) and indications and warnings.
- Navigation safety.
- OE awareness.
- Mission planning and command and control (C2).
- Target intelligence.

1-20. GEOINT is an intelligence discipline that draws on contributions from both the intelligence and engineer communities. Figure 1-2 depicts the intelligence and engineer domains and their alignment with the three elements of GEOINT (imagery, IMINT, and GI). The geospatial engineering contribution to GEOINT includes the standards, processes, Soldiers, and equipment required to generate, manage, analyze, and disseminate the GI necessary to enable understanding of the physical environment. Geospatial engineers manage an enterprise geospatial database that contributes geospatial data to all three elements of GEOINT. Geospatial data are compiled from multiple sources, including the NGA, Army Geospatial Center (AGC), other Services, other federal agencies, and multinational partners, as well as exploiting new collection and production from deployed Soldiers and sensors. In most cases, these data are composed of data layers: elevation matrix data, which are used to depict the geometry of the earth surface terrain; imagery raster data, which are used as terrain texture over the geometry; vector two-dimensional (2-D) and 3-D data, which are used to define the cultural features; and 3-D specific models, which are generally constructed in the high-interest areas. The management of geospatial data is discussed further in appendix B. Geospatial engineering also provides GI that is not intelligence-related, such as safety of navigation; terrain products to support the military decisionmaking process (MDMP); installation maps; and GI&S to support master planning/real estate, range management, and geospatial data for training, modeling, and simulations.

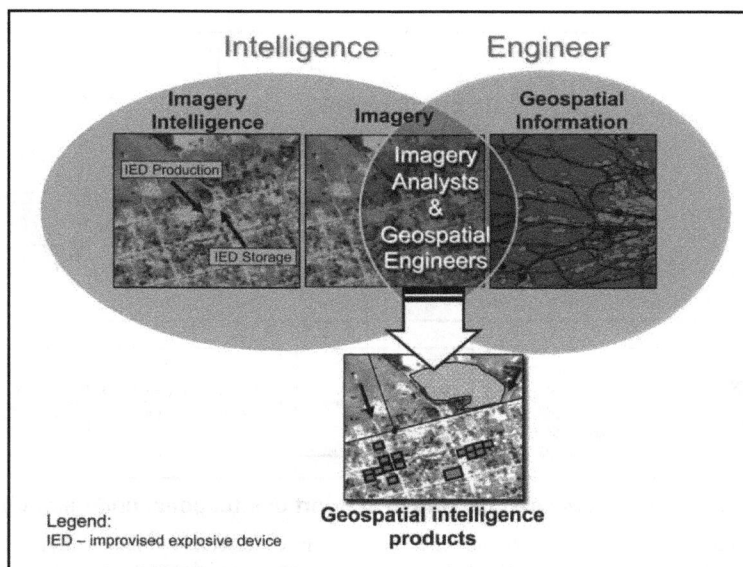

Figure 1-2. The concept of GEOINT

1-21. Army GEOINT cells will form at Army Service component command (ASCC), corps, division, and BCT echelons to provide the commander and staff with the most current, accurate GEOINT analysis and products possible. The GEOINT cell manages the geospatial and imagery foundations of the COP and enables the commander to visualize the operational area. Advances in technology enable the ability to combine the three elements of GEOINT into a single geospatial product, resulting in a more comprehensive, tailored intelligence product for a wider scope of problems and customers. GEOINT cells partner the capabilities of imagery analysts and geospatial engineers, and manage the interface between the intelligence and engineer domains shown in figure 1-2, page 1-7. The GEOINT cell supports joint operations with the following five activities:

- Define GEOINT requirements.
- Obtain mission-essential GEOINT.
- Evaluate available GEOINT data.

- Use and disseminate GEOINT.
- Maintain and evaluate GEOINT.

## SUPPORTING SITUATIONAL UNDERSTANDING

1-22. Commanders use experience, applied judgment, and various analytic tools to gain the situational understanding necessary to make timely decisions in maintaining the initiative and achieving decisive results. As presented in FM 7-15, as part of the Army Universal Task List, support to situational understanding is the task of providing information and intelligence to commanders to help them in achieving a clear understanding of the force's current state with relation to the enemy and other aspects of the OE. Geospatial engineering adds to the commander's situational understanding by improving the understanding of the physical environment, which is integrated primarily through intelligence preparation of the battlefield (IPB), as shown in figure 1-3, but also through other integrating processes that are discussed in chapter 3. ENCOORDs, engineer planners, and geospatial engineers, in cooperation with their counterparts in higher, adjacent, and subordinate units, use analysis and visualization capabilities to integrate people, processes, and tools employing multiple information sources and collaborative analysis to build a shared knowledge of the physical environment. The specific roles and responsibilities of the ENCOORD, geospatial engineers, and other staff members are discussed in chapter 2.

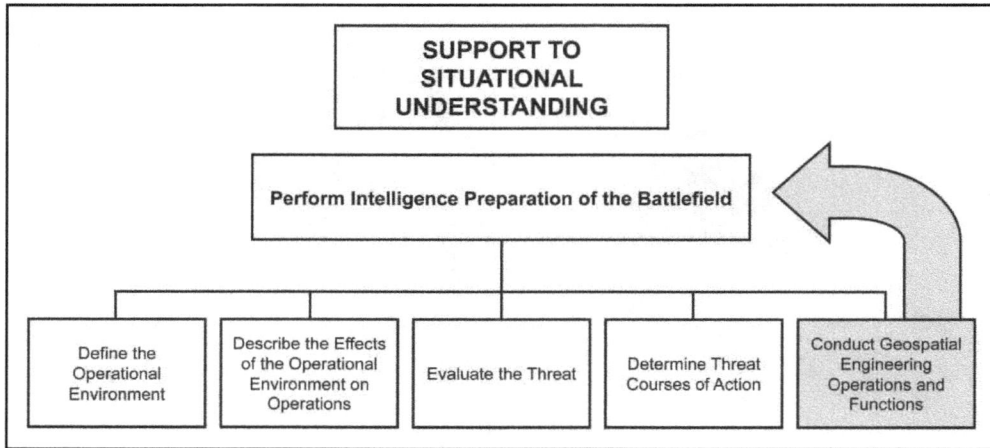

Figure 1-3. Geospatial engineering in support of situational understanding

1-23. The more commanders understand their OE, the more effectively they can employ forces. As described in FM 3-0, today's OEs will likely be set in an urban environment or another type of complex terrain by virtue of an asymmetrical enemy attempting to offset U.S. advantages. *Complex terrain* **is a geographical area consisting of an urban center larger than a village and/or of two or more types of restrictive terrain or environmental conditions occupying the same space. Restrictive terrain or environmental conditions include, but are not limited to, slope, high altitude, forestation, severe weather, and urbanization.** Commanders will depend on several sources of knowledge and RI to understand the complexity of the OE.

1-24. Army doctrine (see FM 3-0) describes an OE in terms of eight operational variables: political, military, economic, social, information, infrastructure, physical environment, and time (PMESII-PT). Each staff section shares a role in providing expertise from their perspective and adding depth and breadth to the overall understanding of the OE. They seek to identify potential challenges and opportunities associated with PMESII-PT and use running estimates to provide RI that commanders can use to frame operational problems.

1-25. Geospatial engineering contributes to the collaborative analysis of the OE by helping the staff better understand and visualize the impacts of the terrain in their areas of expertise. The two primary aspects of the geospatial engineering mission that enable the staff's analysis of the OE and the commander's situational understanding based on the conditions of the physical environment are terrain analysis and terrain visualization, which were previously discussed in this chapter. Geospatial engineering provides the foundational GI on which other information about the physical environment and the other operational variables is based. Geospatial engineers facilitate the staff's analysis of the operational and/or mission variables by describing the physical environment (see figure 1-4, page 1-10).

1-26. The concept of describing the physical environment is initiated by geospatial engineers and other staff specialists in a collaborative analysis of the factors that affect the physical environment (see FM 3-0). Geospatial engineers focus on describing the broad characteristics of the terrain (hydrological, surface configuration, soil composition, vegetation, obstacles, and man-made features), using the framework of OAKOC that will enable a more thorough analysis of the physical environment. As the staff analyzes PMESII-PT, geospatial engineers steadily improve their knowledge of the terrain based on newly generated or acquired geospatial data that enable a more detailed analysis of the terrain's characteristics. As planning progresses, geospatial engineers shape their analysis based on refinement in the commander's intent and added clarity on likely missions. As it is acquired, additional information on the terrain's effects (OAKOC) is disseminated by geospatial engineers to the staff in a combination of written and visual form that corresponds to the warfighting functions (see table 1-3, page 1-11). The staff in turn assimilates that information into their running estimates to assess friendly and enemy capabilities (based on the effects of the terrain) in their areas of expertise and determines the operational impacts from their individual perspectives. The resulting RI is shared within and across echelons to refine the COP and enable situational understanding.

1-27. The GI that is presented (described) to the staff is tailored (formatted) to meet each staff section's needs. Geospatial products can help the staff visually communicate RI to support collaborative planning with higher, adjacent, and lower units and to update the commander throughout the operations process. Advances in technology allow terrain visualization products to be formatted into smaller, more exportable, geospatially aware digital files (such as geospatial portable document format [GeoPDF™]) that can be electronically disseminated to a larger audience.

1-28. Recurring staff requirements for GI and staff preferences for customized geospatial products can be determined based on staff training exercises and operational experiences. Standardizing these staff requirements, especially those routinely needed in certain steps of the MDMP, can help leaders realize the geospatial workload and allow the geospatial effort to be prioritized and sequenced accordingly. This also allows base products to be built ahead of time, maximizing the time available for planning. These products can be periodically reviewed and updated as new information and time becomes available. Capturing these requirements and activities in standing operating procedures (SOPs) will improve staff efficiency and facilitate the training and integration of new staff members.

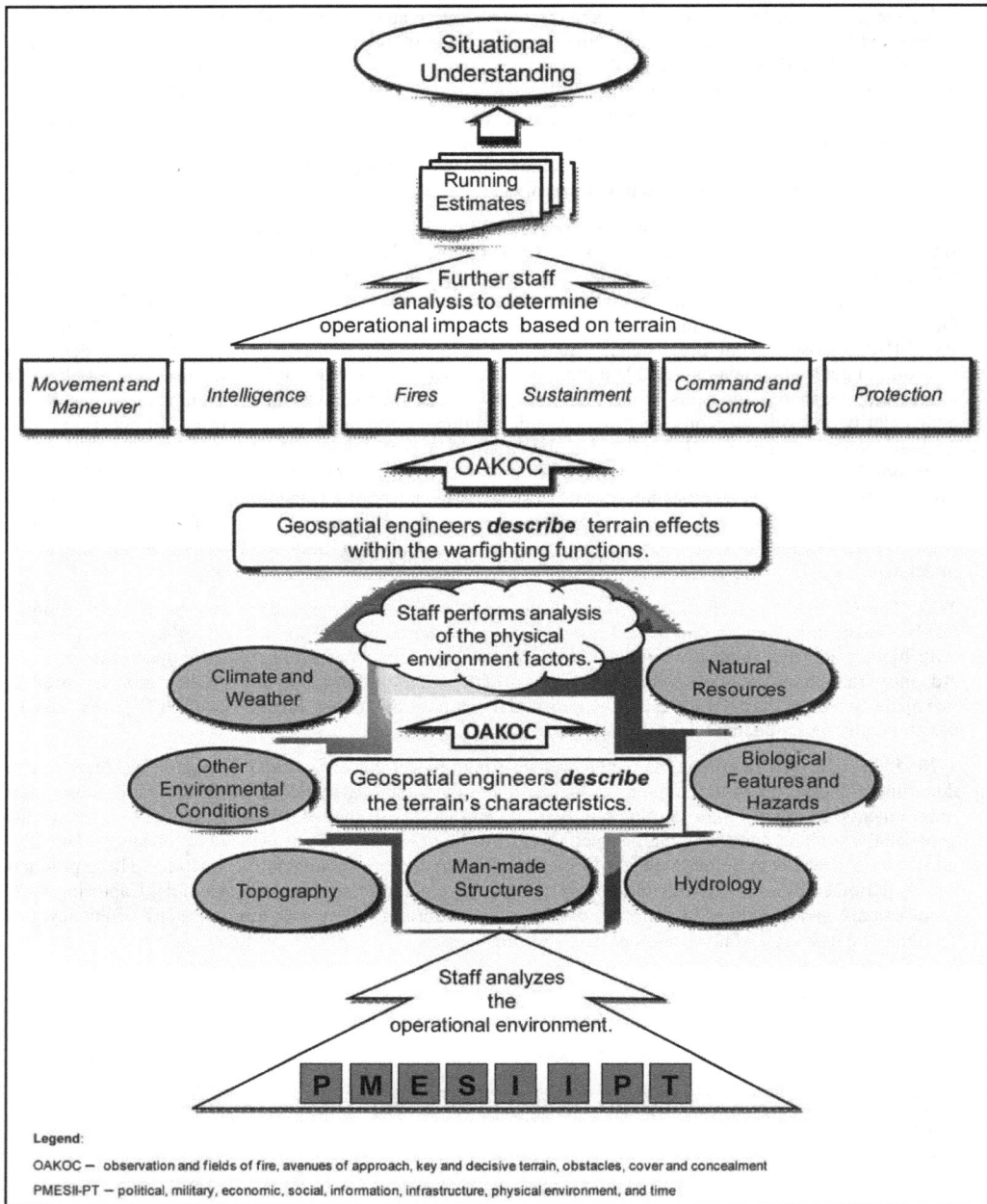

Figure 1-4. Describing the physical environment

**Table 1-3. Geospatial product considerations within the warfighting functions**

| Warfighting Function | Geospatial Product Considerations |
|---|---|
| Movement and maneuver | • Identify mobility corridors and determine AAs.<br>• Predict on- and off-road mobility.<br>• Analyze cover and concealment.<br>• Template helicopter landing zones and drop zones.<br>• Provide LOS overlays for determining patrol routes, observation posts, and potential ambush or sniper locations.<br>• Locate points of penetration and support-by-fire positions in support of attacks and breaching operations.<br>• Identify and analyze potential EAs and obstacle locations based on LOS and fields of fire. |
| Intelligence | • Provide terrain analysis products in support of IPB.<br>• Enable ISR synchronization.<br>• Provide support to targeting (HPT information). |
| Fires | • Facilitate the targeting process.<br>• Template observer and firing points based on LOS and slope restrictions.<br>• Analyze mobility to facilitate repositioning of artillery systems. |
| Sustainment | • Display transportation network (road/rail/air) information for establishing LOCs and main supply routes.<br>• Determine terrain suitability for positioning sustainment capabilities and establishing base camps based on hydrological analysis and assessment of other environmental conditions, such as hazards associated with industrial areas and underground utility lines. |
| Command and control | • Contribute to information superiority.<br>• Establish the foundation for the COP.<br>• Determine terrain suitability (including LOS) for positioning C2 nodes and communication systems. |
| Protection | • Identify enemy air AAs through elevation and LOS analysis.<br>• Provide visibility analysis for implementing protection measures.<br>• Provide cover and concealment analysis for assembly areas and forward resupply nodes. |

**Legend:**
AA – avenue of approach
C2 – command and control
COP – common operational picture
EA – engagement area
HPT – high-payoff target
IPB – intelligence preparation of the battlefield
ISR – intelligence, surveillance, and reconnaissance
LOC – lines of communication
LOS – line of sight

This page intentionally left blank.

## Chapter 2

# Roles and Responsibilities

Though geospatial engineering is an engineer function, its full potential is only realized through a concerted effort of various organizational activities and individual actions at each echelon. This chapter, in a continuation of the discussion presented in FM 3-34, describes key roles and responsibilities for effectively incorporating geospatial engineering in support of Army operations. Refer to JP 2-03 and JP 3-34 for specific information on geospatial capabilities in support of joint force operations.

## ORGANIZATION OF GEOSPATIAL ENGINEERING CAPABILITIES

2-1. In full spectrum operations, Army forces typically operate as part of a joint force and often in a multinational and interagency environment. This environment offers various sources of geospatial engineering, GI&S, and GEOINT capabilities. The characterization of effective geospatial engineering lies in the ability to understand these available capabilities and to effectively go outside the Army engineer community and work with other staff sections, organizations, and agencies. As such, coordination across functional areas focused on supporting various missions becomes critical. This coordination includes the ability to fully define requirements; discover and obtain the necessary geospatial data; put these data into a usable form; and then use, share, and maintain the data with mission partners. Only a cooperative and coordinated effort allows GI to be exploited to the fullest extent possible.

### NATIONAL LEVEL

2-2. The National System for Geospatial-Intelligence (NSG) is the combination of technology, policies, capabilities, doctrine, activities, people, data, and communities necessary to produce GEOINT in a variety of environments. NSG operates within policies and guidelines established by the Director of National Intelligence. The NSG community consists of members of the intelligence community, Services, joint staff, combatant commands, and elements of the civil community. See JP 2-03 for more information.

2-3. NGA, the primary source for GEOINT analysis and products at the national level, produces numerous analytical hard- and soft-copy products and provides standard digital products to include scanned digital maps, elevation data, imagery, and feature data. Units obtain data through the Internet or directly from NGA. DLA distributes hard-copy maps to units. Geospatial engineers can request imagery that can be used for spatial and temporal reasoning or multispectral analysis products that are customized to meet particular operational requirements. Imagery is also used to enhance 3-D and fly-through perspectives. NGA provides an NGA support team (NST) in direct support to each combatant command's joint intelligence operations center. NST has full connectivity with NGA to ensure reachback capability into NGA's total support effort. NGA geospatial analysts may also be attached to units, normally at division level and above, to supplement the organic geospatial engineers and staffs. JP 2-03 provides more information on other national- and Department of Defense (DOD)-level capabilities.

### ARMY

2-4. Geospatial engineering is provided to the Army based primarily on the echelon that is supported. Geospatial engineering is focused on geospatial data generation, geospatial data analysis, geospatial data management, quality control, and data dissemination at the numbered Army and combatant command level. At the corps and division levels, the majority of the workload is required to support geospatial database management, mission planning, and the IPB process. Below division level, geospatial engineering is increasingly focused on current operations and updating the enterprise geospatial database (database management).

2-5. Army geospatial engineer units, supporting each echelon down to the brigade level, provide terrain analysis, terrain visualization, digitized terrain products, tailored map products, map production, geospatial data management, and support to the integration of other GI requirements within the supported force. The organic or augmenting geospatial engineering units available to the commander operate within the command's GEOINT cell. As discussed in chapter 1, the GEOINT cell is composed of imagery analysts and geospatial engineers that provide GEOINT capabilities (GI, imagery, and IMINT). This cell ensures that GEOINT requirements are coordinated through appropriate channels as applicable and facilitates shared access of various domains. The composition of this cell varies based on the echelon and the availability of geospatial engineers and imagery analysts and it is located in the top secret sensitive compartmental information facility. The intelligence staff officer (S-2)/assistant chief of staff, intelligence (G-2) has overall responsibility for leadership of the GEOINT cell. Cell members are supervised by the GEOINT cell officer in charge (OIC) but remain under the command of their parent unit. Within the BCT, the GI technician normally serves as the GEOINT cell OIC. At division and above, either the GI technician or the IMINT technician will serve as the GEOINT cell OIC based on seniority. The key to a successful process is collaboration across functional areas within the headquarters and among the GEOINT cell, higher headquarters, and the rest of the stakeholders.

2-6. The Army has two service centers that support GEOINT: the National Ground Intelligence Center (NGIC) and the United States Army Corps of Engineers (USACE) AGC. NGIC has the mission to produce and disseminate all-source integrated intelligence on foreign ground forces and related military technologies. A major component of the NGIC is the 3d Military Intelligence Center, the Army's only GEOINT battalion. Its mission is to produce and disseminate IMINT, GEOINT, advanced GEOINT, and GI products to the Army, joint, and multinational forces and national-level agencies in support of operational requirements. The AGC has the mission to provide the operational commander with a superior knowledge of the physical environment and support the nation's civil and environmental initiatives through research, development, and the application of expertise in the topographic and related sciences. They produce and disseminate standard and specialized geospatial products and provide technical support and advice to field units.

## CAPABILITIES WITHIN OTHER SERVICES

2-7. A brief summary of geospatial engineering capabilities within the other Services is provided below. See JP 2-03 for more information.

### Navy

2-8. Navy intelligence analysts supported by NGA imagery and geospatial analysts collect, exploit, process, and produce GEOINT as a segment of its all-source production from locations at the Office of Naval Intelligence and the Naval Oceanographic Office.

### Marine Corps

2-9. The Marine Corps has limited geospatial engineering capabilities (that reside in the intelligence branch of the Marine Corps) with one topographic platoon supporting each Marine expeditionary force. Marine Corps GEOINT consists of geospatial intelligence and information, as well as imagery and IMINT. The geospatial intelligence and information aspect of GEOINT is provided by a GEOINT support team assigned to the Marine air-ground task force command element. An imagery detachment, also embedded in the command element, uses tactical, commercial, and national imagery to produce IMINT.

### Air Force

2-10. The Air Force employs two intelligence centers—the National Air and Space Intelligence Center (NASIC) and the 480th Intelligence, Surveillance, and Reconnaissance (ISR) Wing—that perform a host of GEOINT functions. NASIC's mission is to produce integrated, predictive air and space intelligence to enable military operations, force modernization, and policy making. It also serves as the National and DOD center of excellence for foreign air and space intelligence and scientific and technical intelligence. The 480th ISR Wing is the lead Air Force wing for global distributed and reachback ISR, and serves as the Air

Force center of excellence for GEOINT, target analysis, precision engagement, and measurement and signature intelligence. One of the key Air Force responsibilities is to analyze data collected by airborne ISR sensors through the Air Force distributed common ground system (DCGS) ISR weapon system.

# DIVISION ECHELON AND ABOVE

2-11. Theater, corps, and division headquarters are modular entities designed to employ expeditionary forces tailored to meet the requirements of specified joint operations. All three are stand-alone headquarters unconstrained by a fixed formation of subordinate forces. Each is capable of serving as an Army force headquarters. Theater army headquarters serve as the ASCC with administrative control over Army forces and some theaterwide planning and controlling support to joint forces. Divisions and corps are the senior tactical warfighting headquarters, capable of directing BCTs in major operations. Divisions are optimized for tactical control of brigades during land operations. Corps provide a headquarters that specializes in operations as a joint task force (JTF), a joint force land component command headquarters, or an intermediate Army headquarters.

## THEATER ARMY

2-12. The theater army headquarters relies on a task-organized topographic engineer company and/or GPC to provide geospatial engineering support. GPCs are the only units in the Army force structure with unique, dedicated geospatial data-generation capability. Based on the scope of the data-generation mission, the GPCs may be augmented with task-organized topographic engineer company support to enhance their data-generation capability. The topographic engineer company and the GPC require access to the Global Information Grid and classified tactical local area network SECRET Internet Protocol Router Network (SIPRNET) to update and disseminate GI and products.

### Geospatial Planning Cell

2-13. The GPC is the theater geospatial engineering asset that was designed specifically to create geospatial data in support of operations in a single theater. A GPC is attached to each theater army and is usually collocated with the theater MI brigade. This ensures that the GPC has access to data and intelligence and the connectivity it needs to perform its specific mission of generating, managing, analyzing, and disseminating geospatial data, information, and products in support of the theater army headquarters and geographic combatant commander (GCC). The GPC also coordinates with national agencies, multinational and host nation (HN) geospatial support activities, and higher headquarters to create and maintain the enterprise geospatial database.

2-14. The GPC collects, manages, and disseminates the theater geospatial database (TGD) for all units operating in the GPC's area of responsibility (AOR). The GPC enhances existing NGA data, generates new geospatial data, and distributes these data to units operating in their AOR, to include multinational mission partners. The GPC also distributes data to NGA for inclusion in their national geospatial data holdings. The GPC coordinates with geospatial engineer teams across the echelons to ensure a synchronized geospatial data collection effort that is incorporated into the TGD that provides a common database for all users. The organization of the GPC is described in appendix E.

### Topographic Engineer Company

2-15. Topographic engineer companies are force pool assets that can be employed throughout the Army based on mission requirements. Topographic engineer companies provide task-organized geospatial engineering support to theater army headquarters, GPCs, and deployed units that require augmentation. The companies provide modules tailored to support the GCC and JTF headquarters; theater army, corps, and division headquarters; GPCs; modular support and functional brigades without organic geospatial engineer teams; other joint or multinational division and brigade-size elements; and the Federal Emergency Management Agency regions with analysis, collection, generation, management, finishing, and printing capabilities. Because these companies are not controlled by a centralized C2 structure, their effective employment depends on coordination among the parent engineer brigade commander and staff and the Army GI officer, the ASCC GI&S officer, the ASCC ENCOORD or G-2, GPC OIC, and the theater MI brigade commander and staff. The organization of the topographic engineer company is described in appendix E.

## CORPS AND DIVISION

2-16. The modular corps headquarters design, combined with robust communications, gives the corps commander a flexible command post (CP) structure to meet necessary requirements. The corps headquarters has three command nodes—the corps mobile command group, the main CP, and the tactical CP. The corps's two CPs are organized around the warfighting functions and integrating cells.

2-17. The corps and division geospatial engineer team (shown in appendix E) is assigned to the main CP and partners with MI imagery analysts to form the GEOINT cell, which supports the G-2 and the assistant chief of staff, operations (G-3) and other staff sections and subordinate units as directed, to fuse intelligence and GI into a common picture for the commander, staff, and subordinate units. The team collects and provides updated geospatial data and products in support of corps and division operations and performs the following primary tasks in support of the four major geospatial engineering functions:

- Generate.
  - Identify gaps in geospatial data and nominate collection.
  - Acquire geospatial data from multiple sources (such as the NGA and other national agencies, other countries, and other geospatial engineer teams across the echelons).
  - Provide the appropriate geospatial data sets to the ABCS that ensure a common map foundation.
- Manage.
  - Manage the GI requirements process.
  - Manage the enterprise geospatial database that provides the foundation for the COP.
  - Manage the map backgrounds used in the ABCS to minimize inconsistencies and ensure commonality.
  - Monitor collection efforts and verify field-collected data from ISR assets and Soldiers used as sensors, and incorporate these data into the enterprise geospatial database.
  - Manage requests for information (RFIs) aimed at fulfilling gaps in GI.
- Analyze.
  - Perform terrain analysis.
  - Provide terrain products to support decisionmaking.
- Disseminate.
  - Publish and maintain unit geospatial enterprise database server.
  - Disseminate geospatial data in an enterprise environment to ensure that all ABCS users are operating from a common map background.
  - Input field-collected and partner-added geospatial data.
  - Validate, extract, analyze, fuse, and produce relevant data and products for decisionmaking or operations.
  - Integrate and synchronize with other staff.

# BRIGADE-SIZE ORGANIZATIONS

2-18. The geospatial engineer team organic to the BCT, the armored cavalry regiment (ACR), and select modular support and functional brigades perform analysis, management, and dissemination of geospatial data and products in support of mission requirements. It maintains the brigade's enterprise geospatial database on the brigade's server and provides updates to the brigade's portion of the TGD. It validates all information for inclusion in the enterprise geospatial database that is obtained or received from subordinate elements as a result of operations (such as reconnaissance, surveillance, and reconstruction) and analysis of imagery and other source information. The team partners with MI imagery analysts (organic to or augmenting the brigade) to form the GEOINT cell, which supports the S-2, the operations staff officer

(S-3), and other staff sections and subordinate units as directed, to fuse intelligence and GI into a common picture for the commander. The geospatial engineer teams (shown in appendix E) have the capability to—

- Generate and analyze geospatial data.
- Provide terrain products and produce TDAs to facilitate decisionmaking.
- Produce image maps.
- Manage the enterprise geospatial database.
- Manage the map backgrounds used in ABCS to minimize inconsistencies and ensure commonality.
- Operate on a 24-hour basis.

2-19. As discussed in chapter 1, geospatial engineering provides commanders with terrain analysis and visualization, which improve situational awareness and enhance decisionmaking during planning, preparation, execution, and assessment. The geospatial engineer team must have a clear understanding of the mission and commander's intent to ensure a proactive geospatial engineering effort throughout the operations process that is aimed at providing the right information at the right time to facilitate decisionmaking. Applications of TDAs include—

- Promoting the timely development of the modified combined obstacle overlay (MCOO) during IPB to identify AAs, mobility corridors, and chokepoints.
- Enhancing rehearsals with the use of 3-D fly-throughs or simulations.
- Facilitating the positioning and routing of ground and aerial surveillance assets through LOS analysis.

# UNIT AND STAFF RESPONSIBILITIES FOR GEOSPATIAL ENGINEERING SUPPORT

2-20. Geospatial engineering capabilities are task-organized based on mission and PMESII-PT. The ENCOORD is responsible for understanding the full array of engineer capabilities (combat, general, and geospatial engineering) available to the force and for synchronizing them to best meet the needs of the maneuver commander. As previously mentioned, the section of assignment and grouping of engineer staff varies among echelons and unit types. Organization of the assigned staff to meet the unique requirements of the headquarters and situation is ultimately determined by the theater army, corps, or division commander. The responsibilities and functions of Army staff are described in FM 6-0. Joint engineer staff responsibilities are discussed in JP 3-34.

## TOPOGRAPHIC ENGINEER COMPANY COMMANDER

2-21. The topographic engineer company commander coordinates through the parent engineer brigade with the Geospatial Information Office, GPCs, the theater MI brigade, and ENCOORDs and G-2s at the theater army, corps, and division levels to plan and synchronize geospatial engineering augmentation in support of Army requirements. In doing so, the company commander performs the following tasks:

- Coordinates with GPCs or the ASCC G-2 or ENCOORD to ensure—
  - Two-way synchronization and updates for each TGD.
  - Synchronized data-generation efforts in support of each TGD.
  - Deployable modules (augmentation) tailored to meet the ASCC's requirements.
- Coordinates with the corps, division, and brigade to ensure that—
  - Deployable modules (augmentation) include the necessary database management, analysis, and print capabilities to meet requirements.
  - Procedures are established for effectively transferring field-collected data between corps/division/brigade geospatial engineer teams and GPCs.

## TOPOGRAPHIC ENGINEER COMPANY OPERATIONS OFFICER

2-22. The topographic engineer company operations officer coordinates for the deployment of geospatial engineering modules in support of Army requirements. The operations officer also coordinates for rear detachment operations in support of deployed modules.

## ANALYSIS PLATOON LEADER

2-23. The platoon leader is responsible for the leadership of the analysis platoon and for providing effective geospatial engineering support. The platoon leader works with the platoon's GI technician to ensure the training and readiness of the platoon.

## ANALYSIS PLATOON GEOSPATIAL INFORMATION TECHNICIAN

2-24. The GI technician in the analysis platoon trains and supervises the platoon's Soldiers in conducting geospatial engineering operations. The GI technician works with other GI technicians in the GPC and corps/division/BCT geospatial engineer teams to ensure the synchronized transfer of geospatial data among these organizations. The GI technician also performs the following tasks:

- Supervises database management operations and data exchange between the GPCs and deployed modules.
- Manages the deployed units' enterprise geospatial database and ensures that supported unit ABCS operators are using common map backgrounds.
- Supervises terrain analysis performed in support of deployed modules.
- Supervises print operations in support of deployed modules.

## ENGINEER COORDINATOR

2-25. The *engineer coordinator* is the special staff officer, usually the senior engineer officer on the staff, responsible for coordinating engineer assets and operations for the command (FM 3-34). Regardless of the distribution of engineer staff or their section of assignment, the ENCOORD ensures the synchronization of the overall engineer effort.

2-26. Although the S-2/G-2 is responsible for the organic geospatial engineer team and GEOINT cell operations, the ENCOORD remains responsible for the integration of geospatial engineering throughout the operations process and does so by performing the following tasks:

- Plan.
  - Coordinate with the S-2/G-2 for terrain products that will help describe the physical environment to the commander and staff, facilitate a better understanding of the OE, and enable decisionmaking.
  - Provide recommendations on the priorities of geospatial engineering to the S-2/G-2.
- Prepare.
  - Coordinate with the S-2/G-2 for the production and distribution of maps and terrain products based on established priorities.
  - Coordinate for terrain models and products to facilitate rehearsals.
- Execute.
  - Recommend adjustments to the priorities for geospatial engineering based on the situation.
  - Work with the S-2/G-2 to integrate updated GI and geospatial products into integrating processes and continuing activities as necessary (see chapter 3).
- Assess.
  - Establish and maintain a continuous, open link between all engineer cells and supporting engineer CPs to assess the effectiveness of geospatial engineering operations.
  - Work with the S-2/G-2 in assessing the effectiveness of terrain products based on feedback from the commander, the staff, and subordinate units.

## GEOSPATIAL ENGINEER

2-27. Geospatial engineers, in combination with other engineers and other staff members, help analyze the meaning of activities and significantly contribute to anticipating, estimating, and warning of possible future events. They provide the foundation for developing shared situational awareness and improve understanding of friendly forces, capabilities, the adversary, and other conditions of the OE.

2-28. Geospatial engineers use analysis and visualization capabilities to integrate people, processes, and tools, using multiple information sources and collaborative analysis to build a shared knowledge of the physical environment in support of the unit's mission and commander's intent. Geospatial engineers perform the following tasks:

- Plan.
  - Evaluate the availability of standard and specialized maps and imagery products for the operational area or the specific area of operations (AO) and coordinate any shortfalls through appropriate channels.
  - Coordinate the collection of classified and open source GI through reconnaissance, topographic survey, site survey, data mining, and satellite imagery.
  - Submit requests (through appropriate channels) for digital GI from the NGA immediately after mission requirements are determined.
  - Acquire data from multiple sources (NGA, other agencies, and other countries).
  - Process source data (such as imagery, elevation, vector, and textual) into GI and products to populate the enterprise geospatial database.
  - Partner with the intelligence staff to exploit imagery, reconnaissance information and reports, and other collected all-source data to supplement standard terrain databases and to provide geospatial support to the unit.
  - Coordinate with the Air Force weather detachment or staff weather officer to incorporate the effects of current or projected weather conditions into terrain analysis.
  - Perform terrain analysis and provide terrain visualization products in support of the MDMP and the IPB (see chapter 3).
  - Coordinate any created standard data sets back to the national level to update the GEOINT knowledge base.
  - Establish a geospatial product storage and distribution capability in coordination with other staff elements.
  - Establish geospatial policies and procedures.
  - Implement program management for geospatial databases.
  - Coordinate system requirements such as communications, technology, hardware, and software.
  - Publish and maintain the unit's map server.
  - Establish the enterprise geospatial database and continuously update it throughout execution.
  - Ensure that all ABCS users have a common map background.
  - Manage brigade and higher geospatial databases (brigade geospatial database and TGD).
  - Establish and maintain product standards to ensure quality control for database entry.
  - Distribute GI and terrain products to help the staff prepare their annexes and other attachments.
- Prepare.
  - Produce and distribute maps and terrain visualization products based on established priorities to facilitate rehearsals and subordinates' planning.
  - Monitor and integrate the GI being generated through ISR collection, RFIs, and reachback.
  - Respond to new GI requirements being generated as a result of planning refinement and subordinates' planning.

- ■ Continue to manage the map foundation of the COP by ensuring updated and current maps in the ABCS.
- ● Execute.
  - ■ Respond to new GI requirements generated from an ongoing integrating process, continuing activities, adjustments in the commander's critical information requirements (CCIR), or modifications to the concept of operations.
  - ■ Maintain geospatial databases and incorporate new or updated geospatial data resulting from ISR collection, reachback, or unit operations.
  - ■ Produce and disseminate updated terrain analysis products for the staff and subordinate units.
  - ■ Disseminate geospatial data (both digital and hard copy) in an enterprise environment.
  - ■ Facilitate the repositioning of capabilities (adjustments) based on an appreciation of the terrain.
- ● Assess.
  - ■ Advise the commander on geospatial engineering issues.
  - ■ Help the staff to identify and assess variances between the current situation and forecasted outcomes resulting from changes in the terrain due to natural or human influence.

## GEOSPATIAL ENGINEERING TECHNICIAN

2-29. GI technicians are the Army's terrain analysis and GI&S experts. They assimilate and integrate GI to aid the commander and staff in understanding the impacts of the terrain on friendly and enemy operations. As an integral part of the planning staff, they participate in each step of the MDMP to ensure their understanding of the mission and commander's intent. This enables a proactive geospatial engineering effort aimed at providing the right information at the right time to facilitate decisionmaking. They may serve as the OIC of the GEOINT cell, where they work with imagery analysts to produce GEOINT. GI technicians perform the following tasks:

- ● Plan.
  - ■ Integrate geospatial engineering into the MDMP and IPB to describe the physical environment to the commander and staff, facilitate a better understanding of the OE, and enable decisionmaking.
  - ■ Identify gaps in GI for those aspects of the terrain deemed critical during the MDMP and focus the data-generation effort to fulfill those requirements.
  - ■ Coordinate RFIs and nominate ISR tasks through the collection manager to acquire geospatial data such as imagery, elevation, and synthetic aperture radar.
  - ■ Supervise the geospatial engineer team in generating data and performing feature extraction from various sources such as imagery, elevation data, vector data, synthetic aperture radar, LIDAR, and text-based data and reports.
  - ■ Supervise the geospatial engineer team's quality control of geospatial data stored in the enterprise geospatial database.
  - ■ Ensure the quality of the terrain analysis being performed by the geospatial engineer team.
  - ■ Work with the S-2/G-2 in establishing the priorities for the geospatial engineer team throughout the operations process.
- ● Prepare.
  - ■ Manage the production and distribution of maps and terrain products based on established priorities.
  - ■ Provide terrain visualization products to facilitate rehearsals.
- ● Execute.
  - ■ Provide updated GI and terrain visualization products in support of integrating processes and continuing activities as necessary (see chapter 3).
  - ■ Direct the dissemination of terrain products through shared networks and other mediums (digital and hard copy) to meet the requestor's needs.

- Ensure that the enterprise geospatial database is maintained to ensure that ABCS users have a common map background.
- Ensure that geospatial data being collected from the field and other sources are evaluated, compared with the existing database, and incorporated into the new database to provide the foundation for the COP and terrain analysis.

● Assess.
- Manage the collection and management effort of GI.
- Provide GI updates and terrain products in each staff section's running estimate to facilitate their assessment of the situation.
- Continuously assess the effectiveness of terrain products based on feedback from the commander and staff.
- Manage geospatial printing and plotting supplies and request resupply through appropriate channels.
- Establish and maintain a continuous, open link with higher, adjacent, and subordinate geospatial engineer elements to foster effective geospatial engineering operations.

## IMAGERY INTELLIGENCE TECHNICIAN

2-30. IMINT technicians administer, manage, maintain, and operate Army IMINT systems. They may serve as the OIC of the GEOINT cell, where they work with geospatial engineers to produce GEOINT. See FM 2-0 for more information.

## IMAGERY ANALYST

2-31. Imagery analysts exploit imagery from satellite and aerial systems in support of mission requirements. They work with geospatial engineers to produce GEOINT. See FM 2-0 for more information.

## INTELLIGENCE STAFF OFFICER

2-32. Although the ENCOORD is responsible overall for the integration of geospatial engineering, the S-2/G-2 is responsible for the geospatial engineer team and performs the following tasks:
● Plan.
- Integrate geospatial products into the MDMP and IPB to describe the physical environment to the commander and staff, facilitate a better understanding of the OE, and enable decisionmaking.
- Work with the S-3/G-3 and the geospatial engineering technician in establishing priorities for the geospatial engineer team.
● Prepare.
- Monitor the production and distribution of maps and terrain products based on established priorities.
- Monitor and integrate the GI being generated through ISR collection, RFIs, and reachback.
● Execute.
- Adjust the priorities for the geospatial engineer team based on the situation.
- Monitor the distribution of geospatial products to meet the requestor's needs.
- Monitor the maintenance of the enterprise geospatial database to ensure that ABCS users have a common map background.
- Work with the ENCOORD to integrate updated GI and geospatial products into integrating processes and continuing activities as necessary (see chapter 3).
● Assess.
- Monitor the collection and management effort of GI.
- Monitor the supply status of geospatial printing and plotting supplies and coordinate resupply efforts through appropriate channels.

- Continuously assess the effectiveness of geospatial products based on feedback from the commander, the staff, and subordinate units.
- Monitor the provision of GI updates and terrain products in each staff section's running estimate and evaluate its effectiveness in facilitating their assessment of the situation.

## OPERATIONS STAFF OFFICER

2-33. The S-3/G-3 works with the S-2/G-2 in synchronizing the geospatial engineer team's priorities of support and levels of participation in the various functional and integrating cells and working groups in the CP, based on mission requirements and the commander's intent. The S-3/G-3 provides quality control and approves the appropriateness of geospatial engineering-related tasks and coordinating instructions provided in plans, orders, and attachments.

## LOGISTICS STAFF OFFICER

2-34. The logistics staff officer (S-4)/assistant chief of staff, logistics (G-4) is responsible for ensuring the resupply of materials needed for the printing and reproduction of maps and other geospatial products through the appropriate channels.

## PLANS STAFF OFFICER

2-35. The plans staff officer (S-5)/assistant chief of staff, plans (G-5) is responsible for providing general direction to the GI technician, as a member of the planning staff, on the initial GI requirements and terrain products needed to initiate the MDMP. Throughout the MDMP, the S-5/G-5 provides guidance on the quality and nature of terrain products that will best depict those aspects of the terrain that are most important to the commander at a given point in the planning phase, or that will facilitate future planning or the formulation of branches and sequels.

## OTHER STAFF SECTION AND CELL LEADERS

2-36. All staff section and functional cell leaders are ultimately responsible for integrating the results of geospatial engineering within their respective areas. Critical to this role is ensuring that GI requirements are relevant and mission-essential. This prevents overloading the geospatial engineer team and helps focus their efforts. Staff section and cell leaders must clearly communicate their requirements and expectations to ensure that generated geospatial products will meet their intent on the first attempt. They seek out the expertise of geospatial engineers in tailoring products that are both practical and suitable to their needs. Recognizing recurring GI requirements and standardizing terrain products that are typically needed during the MDMP will help manage the geospatial engineer's workload and allow base products to be built ahead of time when time is available. These requirements should be captured in internal staff section or cell SOPs to help train its new members and improve staff efficiency.

## Chapter 3

# Integrating Geospatial Support

Successful integration of geospatial support centers on providing the right GI to the right person at the right time. Doing so requires a thorough understanding of the depth of geospatial resources available, their inherent capabilities, and the ability to recognize opportunities during the conduct of combined arms operations to exploit those capabilities. This chapter focuses on how geospatial engineering is applied throughout the operations process and as a part of the integrating processes.

## THROUGHOUT THE OPERATIONS PROCESS

3-1. As described in FM 3-0, the operations process (see figure 3-1) consists of the major C2 activities performed during operations and is driven by battle command. The cyclic activities of the operations process may be sequential or simultaneous. They are usually not discrete; they overlap and recur as circumstances demand. Throughout the process, the four major functions of geospatial engineering (generate, manage, analyze, and disseminate) are continuously performed to describe the physical environment and the military significance of the terrain, to facilitate the staff's further analysis of the OE, to support situational understanding, and to enable decisionmaking. The ENCOORD performs as the primary staff integrator for all of the engineer functions and works together with the GI technician and the S-2/G-2 in advising the commander to realize the full potential of geospatial engineering.

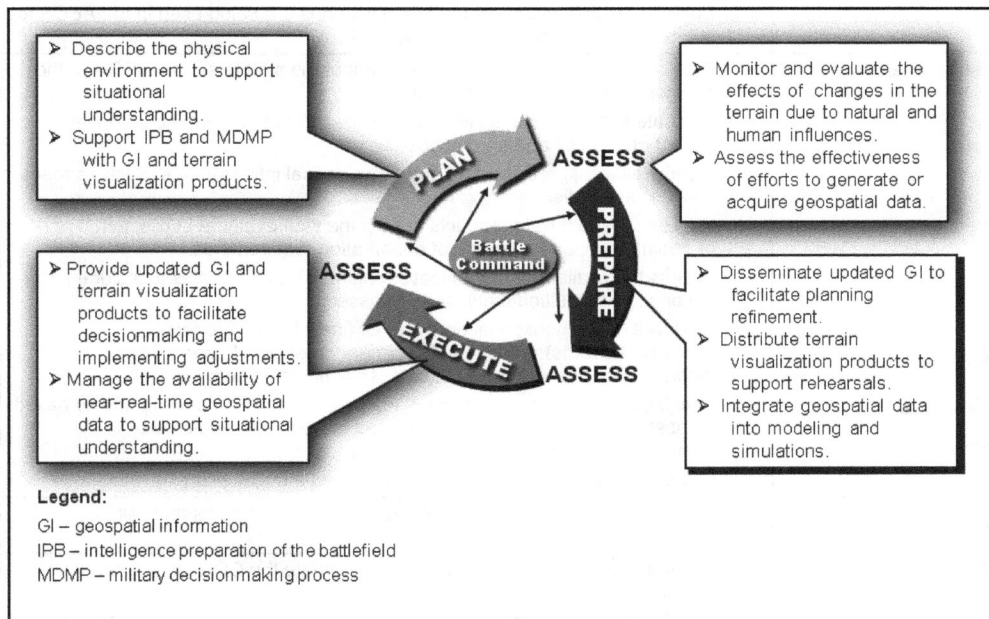

> Describe the physical environment to support situational understanding.
> Support IPB and MDMP with GI and terrain visualization products.

> Monitor and evaluate the effects of changes in the terrain due to natural and human influences.
> Assess the effectiveness of efforts to generate or acquire geospatial data.

PLAN   ASSESS

Battle Command

> Provide updated GI and terrain visualization products to facilitate decisionmaking and implementing adjustments.
> Manage the availability of near-real-time geospatial data to support situational understanding.

ASSESS

PREPARE

EXECUTE   ASSESS

> Disseminate updated GI to facilitate planning refinement.
> Distribute terrain visualization products to support rehearsals.
> Integrate geospatial data into modeling and simulations.

Legend:

GI – geospatial information
IPB – intelligence preparation of the battlefield
MDMP – military decisionmaking process

**Figure 3-1. Geospatial engineering applied throughout the operations process**

PLAN

3-2.   Planning begins with analysis and assessment of the conditions in the OE. In a continuation of the ongoing analysis of PMESII-PT, staffs analyze the current situation using mission variables while preparing their running estimates. Commanders and staffs use the MDMP, described in FM 5-0, to develop the necessary detailed information that will be needed during execution. The MDMP also synchronizes several processes to include IPB, targeting, and risk management, which are discussed later in this chapter. Most of the geospatial engineering effort is integrated into the MDMP primarily through the IPB process (a mission analysis task), as further discussed in Table 3-2, page 3-7. Table 3-1 shows geospatial engineering considerations in relation to the seven steps of the MDMP.

### Table 3-1. Geospatial considerations in the MDMP

| Steps of the MDMP | Geospatial Engineering Considerations |
|---|---|
| Receipt of mission | • Determine the initial GI requirements based on—<br>  ▪ Prominent features of the AO.<br>  ▪ The mission.<br>  ▪ Types of operations likely to be conducted.<br>• Assess the availability of existing geospatial data, GI, and terrain products for the AO by—<br>  ▪ Identifying gaps in knowledge of the terrain that existing maps or imagery cannot satisfy.<br>  ▪ Requesting geospatial data (including geological, climatic, and cultural) and GI from higher headquarters and national agencies through RFIs and reachback.<br>• Disseminate available maps, map products, geospatial data, and GI of the AO to the staff to enable updating of running estimates.<br>• Ensure that correct background map versions are being used in the ABCS to establish the map foundation of the COP. |
| Mission analysis | • Provide GI and terrain products throughout the staff to support IPB and the development of running estimates.<br>• Evaluate terrain, weather, and threat capabilities to determine potential impact on friendly and enemy operations.<br>• Identify available feature data and GI on critical infrastructure (such as roads, bridges, and airfields).<br>• Provide GI and terrain products to help the staff evaluate LOCs, aerial ports of debarkation, and seaports of debarkation requirements.<br>• Assess the availability of geospatial engineering capabilities to include national, joint, multinational, and HN assets.<br>• Review existing geospatial data and GI (including environmental and biological hazards) on potential lodgment areas, reinforced with on-site reconnaissance and infrastructure assessments when possible.<br>• Analyze the mobility restrictions of intervening terrain, including effects based on obstacle intelligence, threat engineer capabilities, and critical infrastructure. Recommend CCIR as appropriate.<br>• Integrate gaps in geospatial data and GI into the ISR effort. |
| COA development | • Integrate terrain products across the warfighting functions that will aid planners in positioning friendly capabilities. |
| COA analysis | • Integrate terrain products that will help evaluate the COAs based on evaluation criteria.<br>• Insert possible changes in terrain conditions (scenarios) into wargaming based on weather effects, such as the loss of a movement route due to surface drainage.<br>• Help planners realize time-distance factors based on movement rates associated with on- and off-road mobility predictions. |

**Table 3-1. Geospatial considerations in the MDMP**

| Steps of the MDMP | Geospatial Engineering Considerations |
|---|---|
| COA comparison | • Use terrain products to help staff sections highlight the advantages and disadvantages of the COAs from their perspective. |
| COA approval | • Provide an update on terrain impacts as part of the current IPB presented during the COA decision brief to the commander.<br>• Determine GI requirements based on the new CCIR to support execution. |
| Orders production | • Provide GI and terrain products to support the staff's development of attachments to operation plans and orders.<br>• Facilitate the production of appendix 3 (Terrain) to annex F (Engineer).<br>• Disseminate GI and terrain products that subordinates will need for execution (continuous). |
| **Legend:**<br>ABCS – Army Battle Command System<br>AO – area of operations<br>CCIR – commander's critical information requirement<br>COA – course of action<br>COP – common operational picture<br>GI – geospatial information<br>HN – host nation<br>IPB – intelligence preparation of the battlefield<br>ISR – intelligence, surveillance, and reconnaissance<br>LOC – lines of communication<br>MDMP – military decisionmaking process<br>RFI – request for information |||

## Generate

3-3.   The generation of geospatial data initiated during planning responds to the gaps in geospatial data coverage identified during receipt of mission. The generation of GI centers on fulfilling the GI requirements established during IPB and those resulting from the staff's analysis of the OE as they prepare their running estimates. Other GI requirements in the form of RFIs will also be generated as a result of subordinates planning in parallel, especially from units at battalion and below that lack organic geospatial engineering capabilities.

## Manage

3-4.   Geospatial databases are established at the onset of planning and are continuously updated and maintained through execution to provide users at all levels with unfettered access to fresh, accurate geospatial data. Geospatial engineers manage the map backgrounds used in the ABCS to minimize inconsistencies. They ensure that correct map editions are being used and that updates are incorporated into the ABCS so that all users are operating from a common map background. The volume of generated GI increases proportionately with the duration of the operation. Unreferenced or stale GI residing in shared folders contributes to information overload and can be misleading. GI must be managed to ensure its effectiveness.

## Analyze

3-5.   As discussed in chapter 1, geospatial engineering aims at describing the physical environment to help the staff further its analysis of the OE. This broad view of the OE is narrowed upon receipt of mission through analysis of the mission variables. Geospatial engineers focus on the characteristics of terrain and its effects on specific aspects of the mission across the warfighting functions. GI enables the overall staff planning effort conducted during the MDMP and planning refinement that continues through preparation.

**Disseminate**

3-6.   GI is systematically disseminated through the ABCS and tactical networks to enable staff planning and the development of running estimates. GI is also disseminated to subordinates in conjunction with the issuance of warning orders to facilitate parallel planning. GI distributed to subordinates should be referenced in orders and relevant to other information provided about the mission to avoid overloading users with information and deterring their own independent analysis. Geospatial engineers also ensure the proper dissemination of new maps and map updates to make certain that all ABCS users are operating from a common map background.

3-7.   During the last step of the MDMP, the staff prepares the order or plan by turning the selected COA into a clear, concise concept of operations with the required supporting information that subordinates need for execution. GI and terrain products are distributed to the staff to help them prepare their annexes and other attachments. Marked improvements in geospatial software and bandwidth capacity have eased the ability to electronically disseminate geospatial products in digital formats (such as GeoPDF files). GI and other information necessary for coordinating and synchronizing the geospatial engineering effort are placed into the appropriate paragraphs in the base order and attachments. The format for appendix 3 (Terrain) to annex F (Engineer) is provided in appendix G of this manual. See FM 5-0 for more information on the general format for orders and attachments.

3-8.   While corps and below Army units normally conduct Army tactical planning, Army forces frequently participate in or conduct joint operations planning. For example, ASCCs routinely participate in joint operation planning, to include developing plans as the joint force land component. Corps and divisions perform joint operations planning when serving as a JTF or Army force headquarters. Corps, divisions, and BCTs, directly subordinate to a JTF, participate in joint operations planning and receive joint-formatted orders. It is important that Army leaders serving in headquarters above battalion understand the joint planning process and are familiar with the joint format for plans and orders. For a detailed explanation of joint operation planning, refer to JP 5-0 and JP 3-33. The primary joint doctrinal publication for planning engineer operations is JP 3-34. JP 2-03 provides the format for annex M (GI&S) to joint orders.

## PREPARE

3-9.   Mission success depends as much on preparation as on planning. Preparation creates the conditions that improve friendly forces' opportunities for success. A key preparation activity is planning refinement based on IPB updates and the answering of information requirements (IR) resulting from ISR collection, RFIs, and reachback. The commander and staff continuously review IPB products against the current situation and redirect ISR assets to focus on the most important unknowns remaining, while emphasizing the CCIR.

**Generate**

3-10.   After issuing plans and orders, new GI requirements in the form of RFIs will be generated as a result of subordinates' planning. The staff will also continue to identify new GI requirements based on its own planning refinement.

3-11.   Geospatial engineering supports mission rehearsals with terrain visualization products such as 3-D fly-throughs and perspective views from projected friendly unit positions resulting from predicted outcomes. Geospatial data are used in modeling and simulations applications in the ABCS and in stand-alone simulation systems to allow commanders to replicate realistic scenarios and facilitate mission rehearsal. To be effective, these applications must represent a realistic physical environment using high-resolution geospatial data.

3-12.   Based on the success of geospatial engineering efforts initiated during planning, the acquisition of new geospatial data and updated GI should facilitate planning refinement and enable the staff's assessment of the current situation using mission variables.

## Manage

3-13. Geospatial engineers monitor and integrate the GI being generated through ISR collection, RFIs, and reachback and continue to update geospatial databases to support planning refinement in preparation for execution. Geospatial engineers continue to manage the map foundation of the COP by ensuring updated and current maps in the ABCS.

## Analyze

3-14. Geospatial engineers analyze newly acquired geospatial data and GI collected through ISR collection, RFIs, and reachback and implement changes to previous terrain assessments used during planning and/or issued to subordinates in mission orders.

## Disseminate

3-15. Geospatial engineers disseminate new or updated GI and terrain products to enable subordinates' mission planning, planning refinement, and execution. They also manage the distribution of new map backgrounds and updates in the ABCS to ensure the integrity of the map foundation of the COP.

## EXECUTION

3-16. Execution is putting the plan into action. It involves monitoring the situation, assessing the operation, and adjusting the order as needed. Commanders continuously assess the operation's progress based on information from the COP, running estimates, and assessments from subordinate commanders. During execution, geospatial engineering focuses on maintaining situational awareness, facilitating assessment, enabling decisionmaking, and promoting responsiveness in implementing adjustments.

## Generate

3-17. As the situation develops throughout execution, geospatial engineers must be prepared to respond to new GI requirements generating from ongoing integrating processes, continuing activities, adjustments in the CCIR, or modifications to the concept of operations.

## Manage

3-18. Geospatial engineers continue to maintain geospatial databases and incorporate new or updated geospatial data resulting from ISR collection, reachback, or unit operations to maintain situational awareness.

## Analyze

3-19. During execution, the priority for geospatial engineering is on the decisive operation. Geospatial engineering helps the staff identify and assess variances between the current situation and forecasted outcomes resulting from changes in the terrain due to natural or human influence. When commanders direct corrective actions (adjustments) based on an assessment of the effects of those variances, the geospatial effort gears toward facilitating the repositioning of capabilities based on an appreciation of the terrain.

## Disseminate

3-20. Geospatial engineers ensure the availability of near-real-time GI through common access databases to allow friendly forces to execute operations at a tempo the enemy cannot match and to act or react faster than the enemy can adapt.

## ASSESS

3-21. During assessment, commanders, helped by their staffs and subordinate commanders, continuously monitor and evaluate the current situation and the progress of the operation and compare it with the concept of operations, mission, and commander's intent. The COP and running estimates are primary tools for assessing the operation. Running estimates, which provide information from the perspective of each staff section, aim to refine the COP with information not readily displayed. The development and continuous maintenance of running estimates drives the coordination among staff sections and facilitates the development of plans, orders, and the supporting attachments. During planning, assessment focuses on understanding the current conditions in the OE and developing relevant COAs. During preparation and execution, assessment emphasizes evaluating progress toward the desired end state, determining variances from expectations, and determining the significance (challenge or opportunity) of those variances.

### Generate

3-22. Throughout the operations process, the geospatial engineering effort is managed to generate the GI that the staff needs to accurately assess the situation. Multiple GI requirements will be generated simultaneously as a result of the ongoing integrating processes and staff actions, requiring prioritization and clarity in purpose of geospatial engineering tasks. In support of simulations and modeling, geospatial data are generated to reflect realistic scenarios and conditions based on the physical environment, which enables future planning.

### Manage

3-23. In support of assessment, geospatial engineers continue to maintain updated geospatial databases and manage the sharing of geospatial data and the flow of GI.

### Analyze

3-24. During assessment, geospatial engineering focuses on helping staffs maintain their running estimates through terrain analysis that highlights the impact of changes in the terrain due to natural and human influences. For example, sudden changes in weather, such as heavy precipitation, may render certain low-lying areas that are vulnerable to flooding (such as wadis, or low-water crossing areas) unusable. Reduced visibility due to fog or dust can impact LOS-based surveillance assets. When adjustments are necessary, geospatial engineering facilitates the repositioning of friendly capabilities with LOS analyses and terrain visualization products. Change detection through temporal analysis of imagery can be used to assess the progress or effects of events or activities that alter the terrain, such as civil-military construction projects, water level adjustments in reservoirs, and agricultural activities. This is particularly useful in areas where the security or political situation restricts a physical presence by friendly forces.

### Disseminate

3-25. Geospatial engineers disseminate relevant GI and visualization products to staff sections, functional cells, and working groups to help the staff evaluate the current situation and the progress of the operation. Geospatial engineers ensure the distribution of new maps and updates to maintain the integrity of the map foundation of the COP.

## WITHIN THE INTEGRATING PROCESSES

3-26. As described in FM 3-0, commanders use the warfighting functions to help them exercise battle command, and they use integrating processes to synchronize operations throughout the operations process. Geospatial engineering is applied across the warfighting functions through various integrating processes, as depicted in figure 3-2 and described in the following pages. Though IPB is primarily aligned with the intelligence function, its role within the MDMP provides a linkage for applying geospatial engineering to each of the warfighting functions.

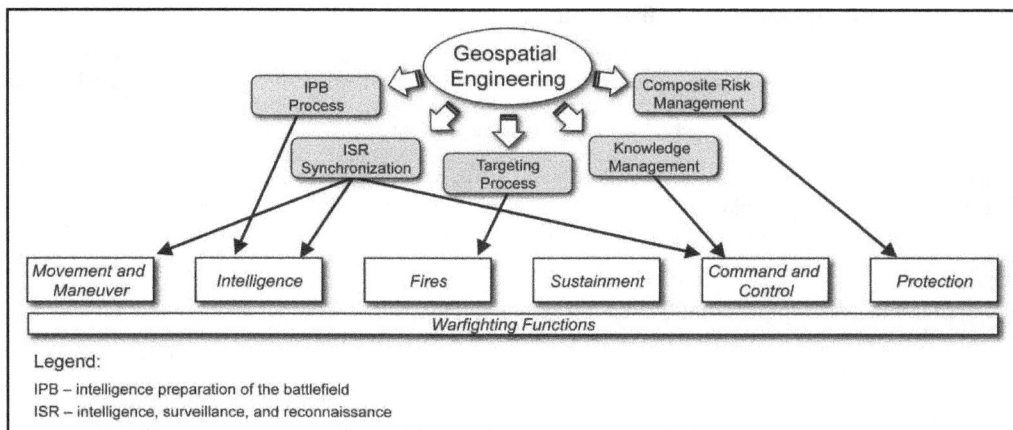

**Figure 3-2. Integration of geospatial engineering across the warfighting functions**

## INTELLIGENCE PREPARATION OF THE BATTLEFIELD

3-27. IPB is an integrating process and occurs during all operations process activities. As described in FM 2-01.3, IPB is a systematic, continuous process of analyzing and visualizing the OE in a specific geographic area for a specific mission or in anticipation of a specific mission. The analysis includes enemy, terrain, weather, and civil considerations.

3-28. Although the S-2/G-2 leads IPB, it involves the entire staff and incorporates information from each section's area of expertise. The integration of geospatial engineering into IPB requires a concerted effort between the engineer and intelligence staffs, as well as coordination and synchronization with higher, lower, and adjacent units. Table 3-2 shows geospatial considerations in relation to the steps of the IPB process.

**Table 3-2. Geospatial engineering considerations in relation to the IPB steps**

| IPB Steps | Geospatial Engineering Considerations |
|---|---|
| Step 1. Define the OE | • Identify gaps in the coverage and the availability of geospatial data and GI for the AO and the AI.<br>• Analyze the factors of the physical environment using OAKOC in consideration of each warfighting function. |
| Step 2. Describe the OE's effects | • Describe the terrain's effects on threat and friendly capabilities. |
| Step 3. Evaluate the threat | • Describe and show the terrain's effects on threat capabilities based on the threat mission or objectives. |
| Step 4. Determine threat COA | • Incorporate GI and terrain products to help pare down the number of COAs based on the terrain's effects.<br>• Describe how the terrain might encourage or discourage one threat COA over another.<br>• Create terrain products (TDAs) that highlight advantages and disadvantages of the terrain against critical aspects of the COA. |
| **Legend:**<br>AI – area of interest<br>AO – area of operations<br>COA – course of action<br>GI – geospatial information | OAKOC – observation and fields of fire, avenues of approach, key terrain, obstacles, and cover and concealment<br>OE – operational environment<br>TDA – tactical decision aid |

## Step 1: Define the Operational Environment

3-29. Step 1 of IPB centers on identifying for further analysis those specific features of the environment or activities in it that may influence available COAs or the commander's decisions. During this step, based on the identification of the area of interest and AO, geospatial engineers identify gaps in the coverage and availability of geospatial data and GI for the AO and area of interest. The engineer and intelligence staffs work closely together to fill these gaps; this includes providing input to the ISR plan, submitting RFIs to higher headquarters, and using reachback to GPCs, national agencies, and other sources. As discussed in chapter 1, geospatial engineers analyze the factors of the physical environment using OAKOC in consideration of each of the warfighting functions. The results of this analysis are then described to the staff as part of step 2.

## Step 2: Describe the Operational Environment's Effects

3-30. Step 2 involves evaluating the effects of all aspects of the OE—with which both sides must contend—and always includes an examination of terrain, weather, and civil considerations. This step consists of two parts: analyzing the environment and describing its effects on threat and friendly capabilities. Geospatial engineering supports this step by describing the results of the analysis initiated during step 1 to the staff. As discussed in chapter 1, describing the terrain's effects on threat and friendly capabilities enables the staff's further analysis of the OE to determine the operational impacts from their perspective.

## Step 3: Evaluate the Threat

3-31. During step 3, threat capabilities are evaluated based on threat missions and objectives. For geospatial engineers, this step is a continuation and refinement of the ongoing terrain analysis, initiated in earlier steps, that remains aimed at helping each staff section better understand the terrain's effects on the threat capabilities within their respective areas of expertise. Geospatial engineers begin concentrating their analysis and evaluation of the terrain's effects based on GI requirements generated by the staff as it collectively furthers its understanding of the threat capabilities. Geospatial engineers incorporate the results of ISR operations, RFIs, and reachback into their analysis and disseminate GI to further the staff's analysis. In a cyclic fashion, as the staff furthers its analysis, the level of detail required to fulfill the staff's additional GI requirements increases as IPB progresses. Geospatial engineers continue to use ISR operations, RFIs, and reachback to augment their own analysis. As GI accumulates within the staffs at each echelon, the management of GI and knowledge about the terrain becomes increasingly important.

## Step 4: Determine Threat Courses of Action

3-32. In step 4, the intelligence staff, helped by the rest of the staff, determines threat COAs based on the analysis performed during the previous steps. The COAs are then prioritized based on the likelihood of their occurrence. Geospatial engineers support this step by providing GI and terrain products that help minimize the number of considered COAs based on the effects of intervening terrain. Terrain suitability products are used to visualize the restrictive aspects of terrain, which can quickly render certain COAs unfeasible based solely on the impacts of the terrain. In prioritizing the threat COAs, geospatial engineers aim at describing how the terrain might encourage or discourage a particular COA over another by assessing the terrain's effects against the COA evaluation criteria, such as the terrain's effects on mobility or rates of march based on threat vehicle capabilities. Geospatial products that visually highlight those advantages and disadvantages of the terrain for each of the COA evaluation criteria can enable decisionmaking, such as cross-country mobility (CCM) and soil trafficability products (see appendix A).

## TARGETING

3-33. Targeting is an integral part of Army operations that determines what targets to attack to achieve the maneuver commander's desired effects and how, where, and when to attack them. The targeting working group uses the targeting process to synchronize the effects of fires, C2 warfare, and information engagement with the effects of other warfighting functions. Geospatial engineering supports targeting with higher resolution geospatial data and products with a greater degree of positional accuracy than TLMs. The full potential of geospatial engineering in support of targeting is best realized through the integration of geospatial engineers within GEOINT cells.

## Targeting Process

3-34. The targeting process is based on four functions: decide, detect, deliver, and assess (D3A). Like other integrating processes, the targeting process is cyclical and occurs continuously throughout an operation. Its steps mirror those of the operations process—plan, prepare, execute, and assess. Targeting occurs in the MDMP and continues after the order is published, validating previous D3A decisions while planning for future decisions. Table 3-3 shows the four targeting functions, the associated targeting tasks, and geospatial engineering considerations within them. See FM 5-0 and FM 6-20-10 for more information on the targeting process.

**Table 3-3. Geospatial engineering considerations in relation to the targeting functions**

| Targeting Process Function | Targeting Task | Geospatial Engineering Considerations |
|---|---|---|
| Decide | • Perform a target value analysis to develop fire support and IE-related HVTs.<br>• Provide fire support and IE input to targeting guidance and targeting objectives.<br>• Designate potential HPTs.<br>• Deconflict and coordinate potential HPTs.<br>• Develop the HPTL.<br>• Establish target selection standards.<br>• Develop the AGM.<br>• Determine measure of performance and measure of effectiveness for BDA requirements.<br>• Submit IRs and RFIs to the S-2/G-2. | • Integrate mobility and suitability products to help template targets and identify potential EAs.<br>• Incorporate terrain effects in calculating HVT movement rates and establishing decision points, timelines, and triggers. |
| Detect | • Execute the ISR plan.<br>• Update PIRs and IRs as they are answered.<br>• Update the HPTL and AGM. | • Perform LOS analysis to help position LOS-based target acquisition assets.<br>• Help update the HPTL based on new GI or assessments of changes in the terrain due to natural or human influence. |
| Deliver | • Execute attacks according to the AGM.<br>• Execute IE tasks. | • Ensure common map backgrounds in the ABCS to enable precision coordinates in deliver (finish) products. |
| Assess | • Assess task accomplishment (as determined by measure of performance).<br>• Assess effects (as determined by measure of effectiveness).<br>• Monitor targets attacked with IE. | • Work with imagery analyst (in the GEOINT cell) in performing change detection to assess effects on facilities and structures. |

**Legend:**

| | |
|---|---|
| ABCS – Army Battle Command System | HPTL – high-payoff target list |
| AGM – attack guidance matrix | HVT – high-value target |
| BDA – battle damage assessment | IE – information engagement |
| EA – engagement area | IR – intelligence requirement |
| G-2 – assistant chief of staff, intelligence | ISR – intelligence, surveillance, reconnaissance |
| GEOINT – geospatial intelligence | LOS – line of sight |
| GI – geospatial information | PIR – priority intelligence requirement |
| HPT – high-payoff target | RFI – request for information |
| | S-2 – intelligence staff officer |

*Decide*

3-35. The decide function is primarily performed during the MDMP. As part of IPB, the S-2/G-2 adjusts threat models based on terrain and weather to create situational templates that portray possible enemy COAs. The S-2/G-2, S-3/G-3, fire support coordinator, and other members of the targeting team collaborate and conduct target value analysis for each enemy COA to identify potential high-value targets (HVTs) associated with critical enemy functions that could interfere with the friendly COA or that are essential to the enemy's success. The completed threat model identifies HVTs, and the situation template predicts their location. Geospatial engineering helps identify HVTs by combining the terrain analysis conducted during IPB with the staff's analysis of the critical enemy functions in each COA and the required capabilities (assets) associated with each function. The staff determines which assets are likely to be of value, based on the enemy's mission and objectives and the conditions of the terrain. Geospatial engineers help the S-2/G-2 assess the importance of those enemy capabilities (assets) based on the conditions of the terrain and predict where they will be employed in the operational area or AO. For example, in an enemy-offensive COA, the prominence of gaps in an operational area or AO could indicate value in threat gap-crossing assets. Further analysis of gap characteristics (such as width and bank height) can reveal possible crossing sites and, when considered in the overall enemy COA, can help the S-2/G-2 template enemy gap-crossing assets.

*Detect*

3-36. The detect function involves locating high-payoff targets (HPTs) accurately enough to engage them and is dependent on the results of the ISR effort. Characteristics and signatures of the relevant targets are determined and then compared to potential attack system requirements to establish specific sensor requirements. Information needed for target detection is expressed as priority intelligence requirement or IR to support the attack of HPT and associated essential tasks for fire support. As target acquisition assets gather information, they report their findings back to the commander and staff. Detection plans, priorities, and allocations change during execution based on the mission variables. The terrain analysis conducted during the decide function is applied within the detect function to help template the location of HPTs and/or predict where they will be employed (based on terrain) to help focus target acquisition assets. For example, artillery slope tint products (see figure A-14, page A-15) can help template enemy artillery positions based on slope restrictions.

*Deliver*

3-37. The deliver function occurs primarily during execution, although some information engagement-related targets may be engaged while the unit is preparing for the overall operation. Geospatial engineering enables precision coordinates in deliver (finish) products by ensuring common map backgrounds in the ABCS. Geospatial engineers integrate the results of terrain analysis in determining types of munitions and delivery means, based on the terrain's effects.

*Assess*

3-38. The assess function occurs throughout the operations process but is most intense during execution. Battle damage assessment (BDA) is the timely and accurate estimate of damage resulting from attacks on targets. Geospatial engineers work with imagery analysts in the GEOINT cell in performing change detection, which can be used to assess effects on facilities and structures.

## Targeting Meetings

3-39. During execution, the targeting working group continually assesses the current situation, tracks decision points, prepares update briefs for the commander, and looks toward the future. The targeting meeting provides a forum for extending the fire support planning that was conducted during the MDMP throughout the operation, allowing the targeting working group to reconsider "who-kills-whom" decisions and modify or initiate actions to implement those decisions. The targeting meeting is an important event in the CP battle rhythm. It focuses and synchronizes the unit's combat power and resources toward finding, tracking, attacking, and assessing HPTs. The integration of geospatial engineering in targeting meetings can help to—

- Update the high-payoff target list (HPTL) based on new GI or an assessment of changes in the terrain due to natural or human influence.
- Position or shift LOS-based target acquisition assets based on terrain restrictions.
- Determine the suitability of lethal and nonlethal delivery systems based on the terrain.
- Determine effects and BDA based on change detection through temporal analysis of imagery.

3-40. The keys to successful targeting meetings are preparation and focus. Each representative must come to the meeting prepared to discuss available assets, capabilities, and limitations related to their staff area. Much of this preparation will require time-consuming, detailed planning and coordination with other staff sections well in advance. Before the targeting meeting, the ENCOORD, the GI technician, and the S-2/G-2 work to—

- Gather available GI pertaining to potential HPT nominations and where they may be employed, based on the terrain.
- Provide GI that could impact the means of delivery, munitions used, or the placement of scatterable mines to reinforce existing terrain.
- Make recommendations for air tasking-order nominations (normally based on a 72-hour cycle) for the employment of fixed-wing imagery assets.
- Provide updates on the terrain's effects based on changes in the terrain due to natural or human influence or the acquisition of new GI resulting from refined terrain analysis, ISR collection, RFIs, and reachback.
- Be prepared to provide GI and geospatial products pertaining to the restricted target list.

## INTELLIGENCE, SURVEILLANCE, AND RECONNAISSANCE SYNCHRONIZATION

3-41. ISR operations contribute significantly to the commander's visualization and decisionmaking. Through ISR, commanders and staffs continuously plan, task, and employ collection assets and forces. These assets and forces collect, process, and disseminate timely and accurate combat information—and intelligence to satisfy the CCIR and other intelligence requirements. ISR synchronization is one of the four tasks of ISR. *Intelligence, surveillance, and reconnaissance synchronization* is the task that accomplishes the following: analyzes information requirements and intelligence gaps; evaluates available assets internal and external to the organization; determines gaps in the use of those assets; recommends ISR assets controlled by the organization to collect on the CCIR; and submits RFIs for adjacent and higher collection support (FM 3-0). ISR synchronization is continuous and is used to assess ISR reporting. FMI 2-01 provides doctrine on ISR synchronization. See FM 2-0, FM 3-20.96, FM 3-90.5, and FM 3-90.6 for more information on ISR operations.

3-42. ISR synchronization satisfies as many IRs as possible through staff coordination and RFIs. Although ISR synchronization is within the intelligence warfighting function, it requires the entire staff's participation to facilitate its integration. Geospatial engineering is integrated into ISR synchronization through ISR working groups, GEOINT cells, running estimates, and the ISR synchronization process. Table 3-4, page 3-12, shows geospatial engineering considerations in each of the six nonsequential steps of the ISR synchronization process. As with other integrating processes, the ENCOORD is the staff officer responsible for integrating the engineer functions in ISR synchronization. Working with geospatial engineers, the ENCOORD advises the S-2/G-2 and S-3/G-3 on the geospatial engineering and engineer reconnaissance capabilities available and how best to use them. See FM 3-34.170 for more information on engineer reconnaissance.

**Table 3-4. Geospatial engineering considerations in the ISR synchronization process**

| ISR Synchronization Process Steps | Geospatial Engineering Considerations |
|---|---|
| Develop requirements | <ul><li>Determine GI requirements based on—<ul><li>Commander's initial guidance for initial IR or CCIR as part of receipt of mission.</li><li>Staff-generated IR during mission analysis.</li><li>Running estimate updates.</li><li>Updates to the CCIR.</li></ul></li><li>Determine the best ways to satisfy GI requirements, including RFIs, reachback, and tasking ISR assets.</li><li>Prioritize GI requirements based on the mission and the commander's intent, to focus geospatial engineering assets.</li></ul> |
| Develop ISR synchronization plan | <ul><li>Understand the capability of the various ISR assets that can provide geospatial data and GI, and provide input in ISR tasks and RFIs being developed.</li><li>Help the staff evaluate the capabilities (such as range) of available ISR assets, based on terrain effects.</li><li>Estimate movement rates of ground ISR assets, based on mobility predictions to help determine employment timelines and determine triggers.</li></ul> |
| Support ISR integration | <ul><li>Support ISR planning and tasking with terrain analysis and visualization products.</li><li>Provide GI and terrain products throughout the base order and annexes that support the ISR plan (annex L).</li></ul> |
| Disseminate | <ul><li>Update and maintain geospatial databases to provide common access to current geospatial data.</li><li>Ensure the distribution of new maps and updates to maintain the integrity of the map foundation of the COP.</li><li>Develop systems and determine procedures for tracking GI requirements and disseminating GI.</li></ul> |
| Assess ISR operations | <ul><li>Monitor the status of ISR tasks pertaining to GI requirements.</li><li>Evaluate reports and feeds to determine accuracy and relevance of GI and geospatial data.</li><li>Determine the effectiveness of ISR assets tasked to fulfill GI requirements and recommend retasking other collection assets as necessary.</li><li>Provide feedback through appropriate channels on the effectiveness of ISR assets and the results of reachback.</li></ul> |
| Update ISR operations. | <ul><li>Eliminate satisfied GI requirements from the ISR plan.</li><li>Integrate new GI requirements into the ISR plan as necessary.</li><li>Recommend adjustments to the ISR plan to fulfill unsatisfied GI requirements that remain relevant.</li><li>Conduct LOS analysis to help in redirecting ISR collection efforts based on changes in terrain and weather conditions.</li></ul> |

| Legend: | |
|---|---|
| CCIR – commander's critical information requirement | IR – intelligence requirement |
| | ISR – intelligence, surveillance, and reconnaissance |
| COP – common operational picture | LOS – line of sight |
| GI – geospatial information | RFI – request for information |

3-43. Terrain analysis and evaluation of the terrain's effects help the intelligence staff employ collection assets that allow maximum effectiveness without exposing those assets to unacceptable risks. Terrain can mask a target from direct observation or restrict mobility of the ISR asset. Elevation analysis can help in positioning LOS-based ISR assets. Evaluating the cover and concealment provided by the terrain can help in determining which routes offer the best survivability based on the protection needs of the ISR asset.

3-44. The staff collectively determines IRs during IPB that will focus ISR operations in generating intelligence to support the mission. In a cooperative effort between the intelligence and engineer staffs, IRs are analyzed to determine which ones can be fulfilled through geospatial engineering—including reachback through appropriate channels to GPCs and national-level assets such as the NGA and the AGC.

## GEOSPATIAL ENGINEERING IN OTHER INTEGRATING PROCESSES

### Composite Risk Management

3-45. Composite risk management (CRM) is an integrating process and occurs during all operations process activities. CRM is the process of identifying, assessing, and controlling hazards (risks) that arise from operational factors and balancing that risk with mission benefits (see FM 5-19). CRM helps to preserve the force and is integrated primarily through the MDMP during planning and through protection cells or working groups throughout the rest of the operations process. Table 3-5, page 3-14, shows the five steps of the CRM process with geospatial engineering considerations for each step.

3-46. During mission analysis, the focus is on performing the first two steps, which concern assessment. Hazards are identified using mission variables as a standard format. Geospatial engineering focuses on helping the staff to visualize and assess those hazards associated with the physical environment. Geospatial engineers consider the factors discussed in chapter 1 that affect the physical environment. Risk is then assigned to each hazard in terms of probability and severity. Step 3 (develop controls and make risk decisions) is accomplished during COA development, COA analysis, COA comparison, and COA approval. Geospatial engineering can aid planners in determining the effectiveness of cover and concealment provided by natural and man-made features along movement routes and in static positions. Controls are implemented (step 4) through mission orders, mission briefings, running estimates, and SOPs. Geospatial engineers can create special-purpose maps and visualization products (such as image maps with annotations) to help leaders communicate their instructions. Step 5 (supervise and evaluate) is conducted continuously throughout the operations process. See FM 5-19 for more information on CRM.

**Table 3-5. Geospatial engineering considerations in relation to the CRM steps**

| Composite Risk Management Steps | Geospatial Engineering Considerations |
|---|---|
| Identify hazards. | • Analyze and describe to the staff those hazards associated with the physical environment. |
| Assess hazards to determine risks. | • Assign risk to each hazard in terms of probability and severity. |
| Develop controls and make risk decisions. | • Determine how terrain (cover and concealment) can be used effectively to enhance survivability. |
| Implement controls. | • Provide appropriate input into mission orders, briefings, running estimates, and SOPs as necessary. |
| Supervise and evaluate. | • Assess the effectiveness of geospatial engineering applied throughout the CRM process, and provide feedback to leaders. |
| **Legend:**<br>CRM – composite risk management<br>SOP – standing operating procedure | |

## Knowledge Management

3-47. Given the complexity and dynamic nature of today's OEs, information must become knowledge that permeates throughout the Army to enable timely decisionmaking. Knowledge management (KM) is the art of gaining and applying information throughout the Army using people, processes, and technology. It generates knowledge products and services by and among commanders and staffs. It supports collaboration and the conduct of operations while improving organizational performance. See FM 6-01.1 for more information on KM, the KM process, and the roles of the KM section.

3-48. Geospatial engineers apply KM to effectively transfer their knowledge of the physical environment gained through terrain analysis. They work with the KM section, specifically content managers, to implement effective means to apply GI and share knowledge of the terrain to further the staff's analysis of the OE and enable the commander's situational understanding. Geospatial engineers break down geospatial stovepipes and provide multiple users with rapid accessibility and retrieval of relevant GI that is enabled through effective management of geospatial databases and the map foundation of the COP. They facilitate a near-real-time, collaborative, information-sharing environment by exploiting information systems, knowledge networks, and tactical Web portals.

# Appendix A

# Geospatial Products

Geospatial products are visual representations of RI pertaining to the terrain's effects derived from terrain analysis. They contain information about the physical environment that can be easily understood by commanders and staffs to help them better understand their OE and enable decisionmaking. This appendix provides an overview of the standard geospatial products provided by national agencies and the tailored products generated by geospatial engineers.

## STANDARD GEOSPATIAL PRODUCTS

A-1. Standard products (paper and digital maps) are created by NGA and the United States Geological Survey. Scanned maps are simply paper maps that have been scanned into a computer file. There are two types of scanned maps that are produced by NGA: arc-digitized raster graphics and CADRG. The AGC also provides NGA maps in GeoPDF format.

### JOINT OPERATIONAL GRAPHIC–AIR

A-2. Joint operational graphic–air (JOG–A) (see figure A-1) charts are medium scale maps modified for aeronautical use. The JOG–A displays topographic data such as relief, drainage, vegetation, and populated areas and includes an aeronautical overprint depicting obstructions, aerodromes, special use airspace, navigational aids, and related data. JOG–A maps support tactical and other air activities including low-altitude visual navigation.

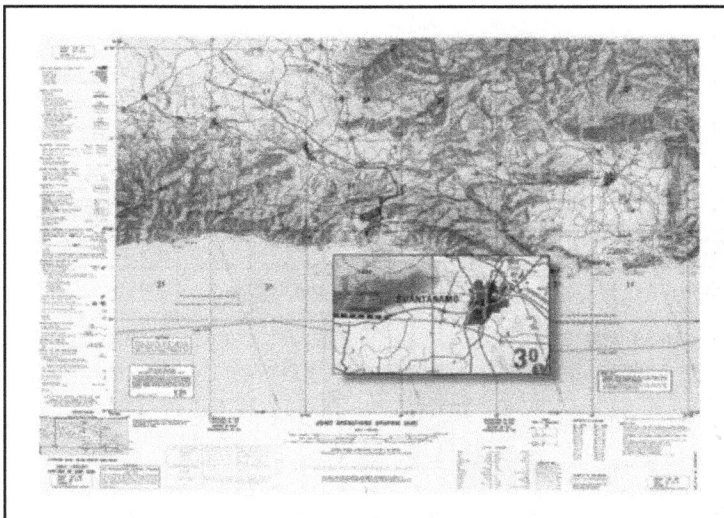

Figure A-1. Example of a JOG–A map (1:250,000)

## TOPOGRAPHIC LINE MAP

A-3. There is not TLM coverage for the entire world. Requirements for NGA production of TLMs are based on theater commander requirements.

A-4. A 1:50,000-scale TLM (see figure A-2) is the standard map used for dismounted tactical planning and operations. A 1:100,000-scale map is more commonly used for mounted planning and operations and is better suited in areas with less significant terrain features and when movement can be conducted rapidly across the area.

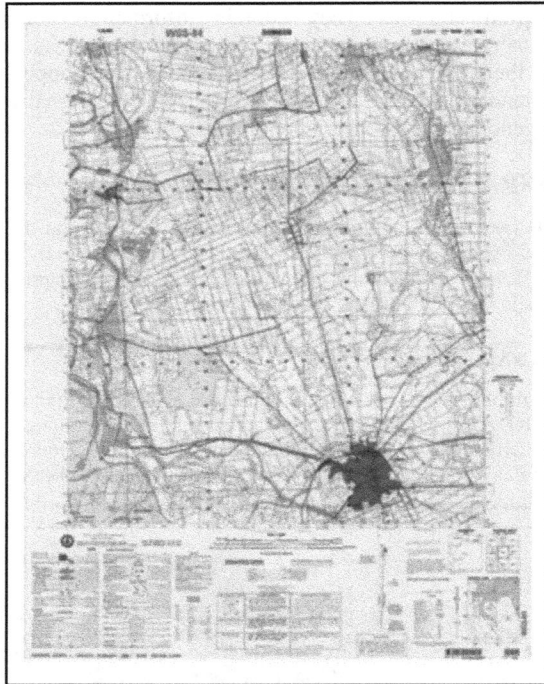

**Figure A-2. Example of a TLM (1:50,000)**

## CITY GRAPHIC MAP

A-5. The scales of city graphic maps generally range from 1:10,000 to 1:35,000, depending on the size of the city. This large-scale product is used for planning and conducting ground combat operations in urban areas. It depicts street names; traffic networks; port facilities; airfields; individual buildings; military, industrial and governmental complexes; hospitals; schools; places of worship; and other key features.

# TAILORED PRODUCTS

A-6. Geospatial engineers create tailored products that combine or integrate matrix, raster, and vector information (see table A-1). The following are examples of products that geospatial engineers can tailor to support mission planning, preparation, execution, and assessment. These products are generated digitally and consist of base imagery, map, or elevation background with various layers overlaid on top. These digital layers have database tables associated with each component that allows them to be queried, analyzed, and displayed to create the desired end product. Because they are digital overlay files, they can be displayed in any number of ABCS.

## Table A-1. Examples of tailored geospatial products

| Geospatial Product | Primary Uses |
|---|---|
| CCM (figure A-3, page A-4) | • Identifies mobility corridors and friendly and enemy AAs and EAs. |
| Linear obstacles (figure A-4, page A-5) | • Portrays linear obstacles that impede mobility.<br>• Combines with CCM to create a COO. |
| Combined obstacle overlay (figure A-5, page A-6) | • Identifies mobility corridors and friendly and enemy AAs and EAs. |
| Mobility corridors (figure A-6, page A-7) | • Shows mobility corridors by combining CCM, transportation and linear obstacle overlays. |
| LOCs (figure A-7, page A-8) | • Identifies available road and transportation networks in an operational area or AO. |
| Hydrology analysis (figure A-8, page A-9) | • Shows the operational impacts of water features in an operational area or AO. |
| Drop zones (figure A-9, page A-10) | • Locates possible drop zones in an operational area or AO to support airborne operations. |
| Helicopter landing zones (figure A-10, page A-11) | • Locates possible landing zones in an operational area or AO to support air assault operations. |
| Vegetation analysis (figure A-11, page A-12) | • Determines the suitability of an area (such as cover and concealment, mobility restrictions) based on the effects of the vegetation in an operational area or AO. |
| Soil trafficability (figure A-12, page A-13) | • Shows the effects of soil on trafficability. |
| Field of fire (figure A-13, page A-14) | • Locates defensible terrain in an operational area or AO.<br>• Identifies possible EAs and position fighting systems. |
| Artillery slope tint (figure A-14, page A-15) | • Templates enemy artillery assets based on slope restrictions. |
| Aerial concealment (figure A-15, page A-16) | • Shows areas or routes that offer concealment from overhead detection. |
| Surface material (figure A-16, page A-17) | • Depicts areas based on types of soil that constitute its surface.<br>• Provides information on trafficability, construction projects, and survivability (dig/slow-dig overlays). |
| Construction resources (figure A-17, page A-18) | • Shows areas that contain certain types of materials to support construction planning. |
| Shaded relief (figure A-18, page A-19) | • Highlights variations in elevation and slope in an operational area or AO. |
| LOS analysis (figure A-19, page A-20) | • Shows areas of direct observation from a given point that can help position LOS-based systems. |
| Perspective view (figure A-20, page A-21) | • Provides 3-D terrain visualization from an observer's point of view. |
| Fly-through (figure A-21, page A-22) | • Provides 3-D terrain visualization of an area that could be seen from an aircraft. |
| UTP (figure A-22, page A-23) | • Displays key aspects of urban terrain to facilitate operating in an urban environment. |

| Legend: | | | |
|---|---|---|---|
| 3-D | three-dimensional | COO | combined obstacle overlay |
| AA | avenue of approach | EA | engagement area |
| AO | area of operations | LOC | lines of communication |
| CCM | cross-country mobility | LOS | line of sight |
| | | UTP | Urban Tactical Planner™ |

CROSS-COUNTRY MOBILITY

A-7. The CCM product (see figure A-3) demonstrates the off-road speed for a vehicle as determined by the terrain (soil, slope, and vegetation) and the vehicle's performance capabilities; however, it does not consider the effects of roads and obstacles. The CCM is used to help identify AAs and engagement areas (EAs).

1:250,000
Zagros Mountains, Iraq
DTED2
Shaded Relief

**Legend**

■ Severely Restricted

□ Restricted

▨ Unrestricted

Surface Condition: Wet
Slippery Condition: Slippery
Water Level: Medium
Historical Rain Fall Information: January

**Figure A-3. Example of a product showing CCM**

## LINEAR OBSTACLE OVERLAY

A-8. The linear obstacle overlay (see figure A-4) portrays linear natural or man-made terrain features (such as escarpments, embankments, road cuts and fills, depressions, fences, walls, hedgerows, pipelines, bluffs, and moats) that pose as obstacles. This information can be combined with a CCM product to create a combined obstacle overlay (COO).

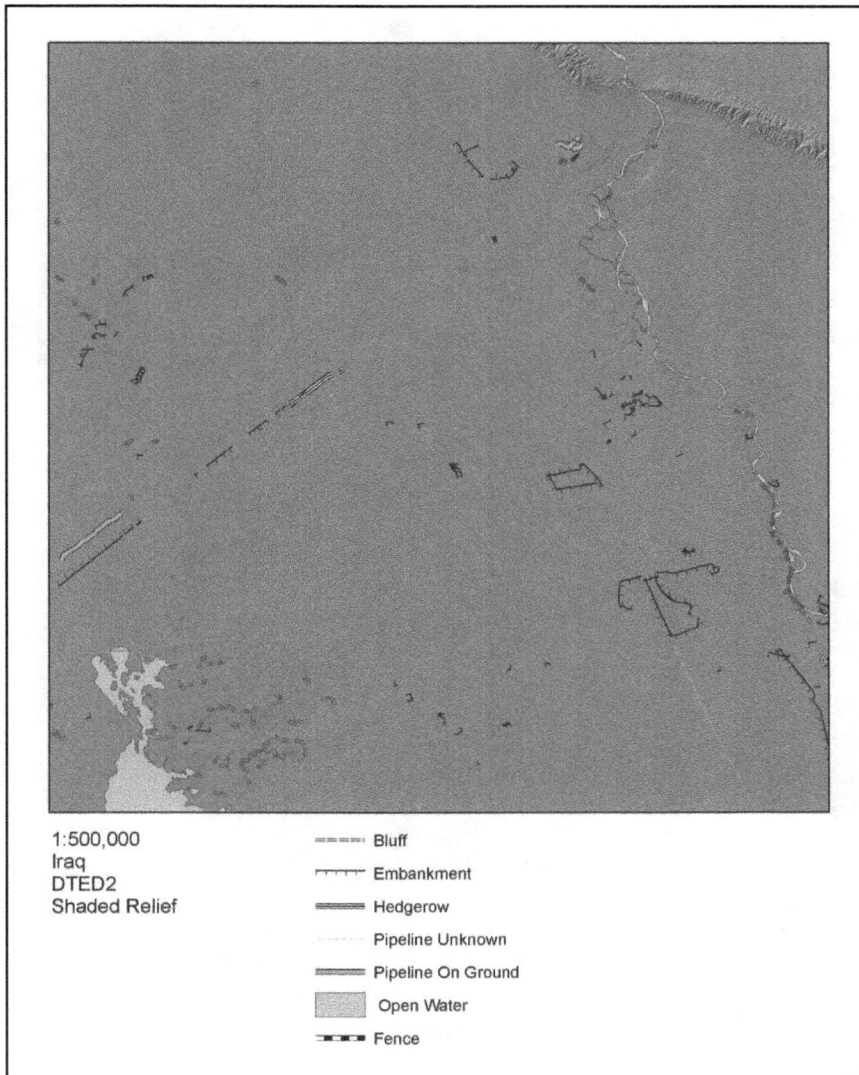

1:500,000
Iraq
DTED2
Shaded Relief

===== Bluff
⌐⌐⌐⌐ Embankment
===== Hedgerow
········· Pipeline Unknown
===== Pipeline On Ground
▓▓▓ Open Water
■━■━■ Fence

**Figure A-4. Example of a product showing linear obstacles**

## COMBINED OBSTACLE OVERLAY

A-9. The COO (see figure A-5) provides a basis for identifying ground AAs and mobility corridors. Unlike the CCM, the COO integrates all obstacles to vehicular movement such as built-up areas, slope, soils, vegetation, and hydrology into one overlay. The overlay depicts areas that impede movement (severely restricted and restricted areas) and areas where friendly and enemy forces can move unimpeded (unrestricted areas).

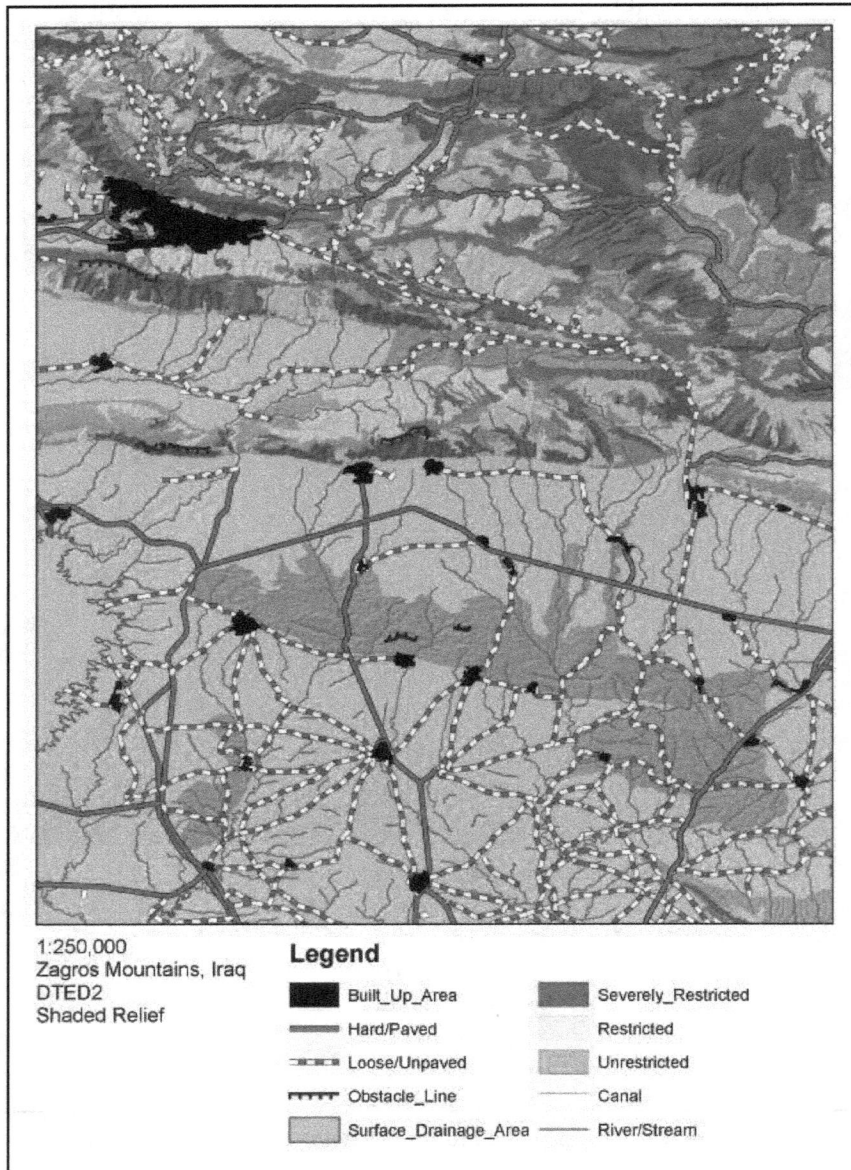

**Figure A-5. Example of COO linear obstacles**

## MOBILITY CORRIDORS

A-10. This product (see figure A-6) is a combination of CCM, transportation, and linear obstacle overlays to show mobility corridors that are based on the restrictiveness of the terrain, vehicle capabilities, and preferred movement formations. This product is used to identify AAs, plan movements, and develop EAs.

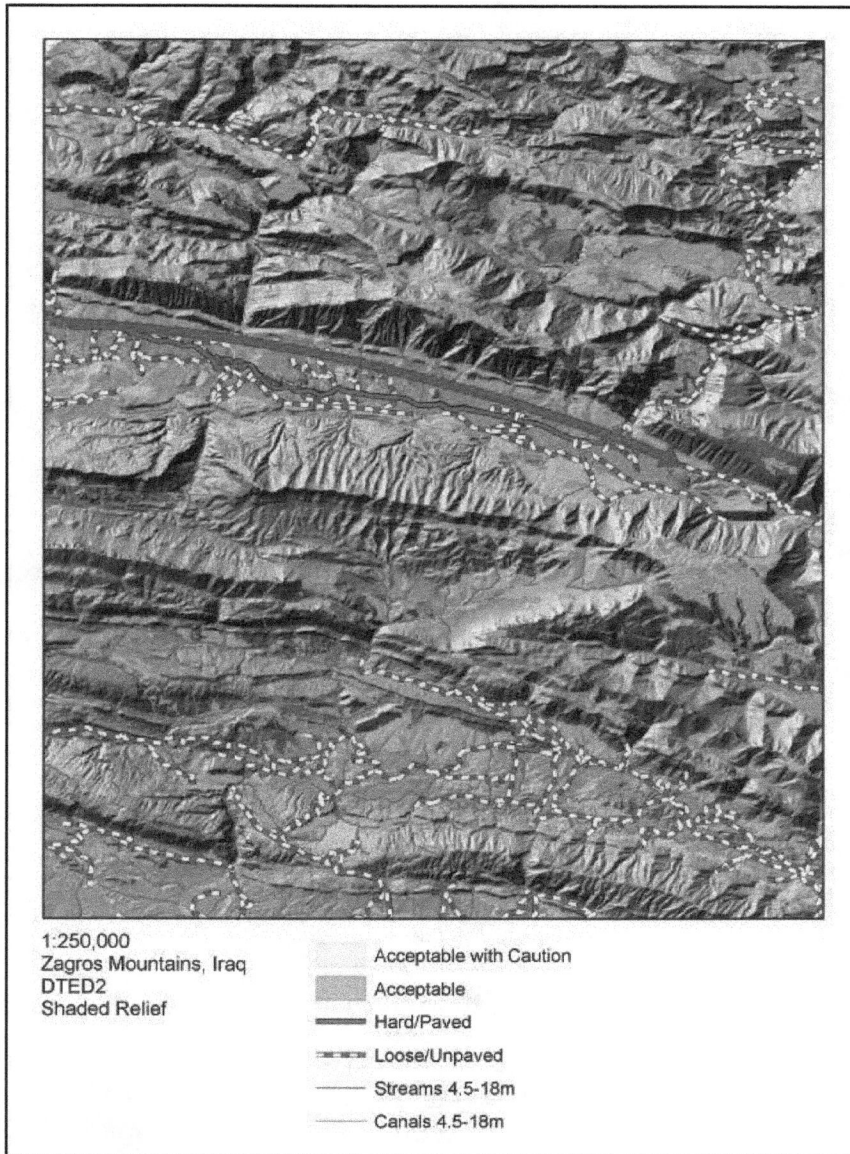

1:250,000
Zagros Mountains, Iraq
DTED2
Shaded Relief

Acceptable with Caution
Acceptable
Hard/Paved
Loose/Unpaved
Streams 4.5-18m
Canals 4.5-18m

**Figure A-6. Example of a product showing mobility corridors**

## LINES OF COMMUNICATION OVERLAY

A-11. The lines of communication (LOCs) overlay (see figure A-7) shows all routes in an operational area, to include dual highways, all-weather hard and loose surface roads, footpaths, airfields, railroads, bridges, ferries, docks, and other man-made features that are used for transporting people, goods, and equipment.

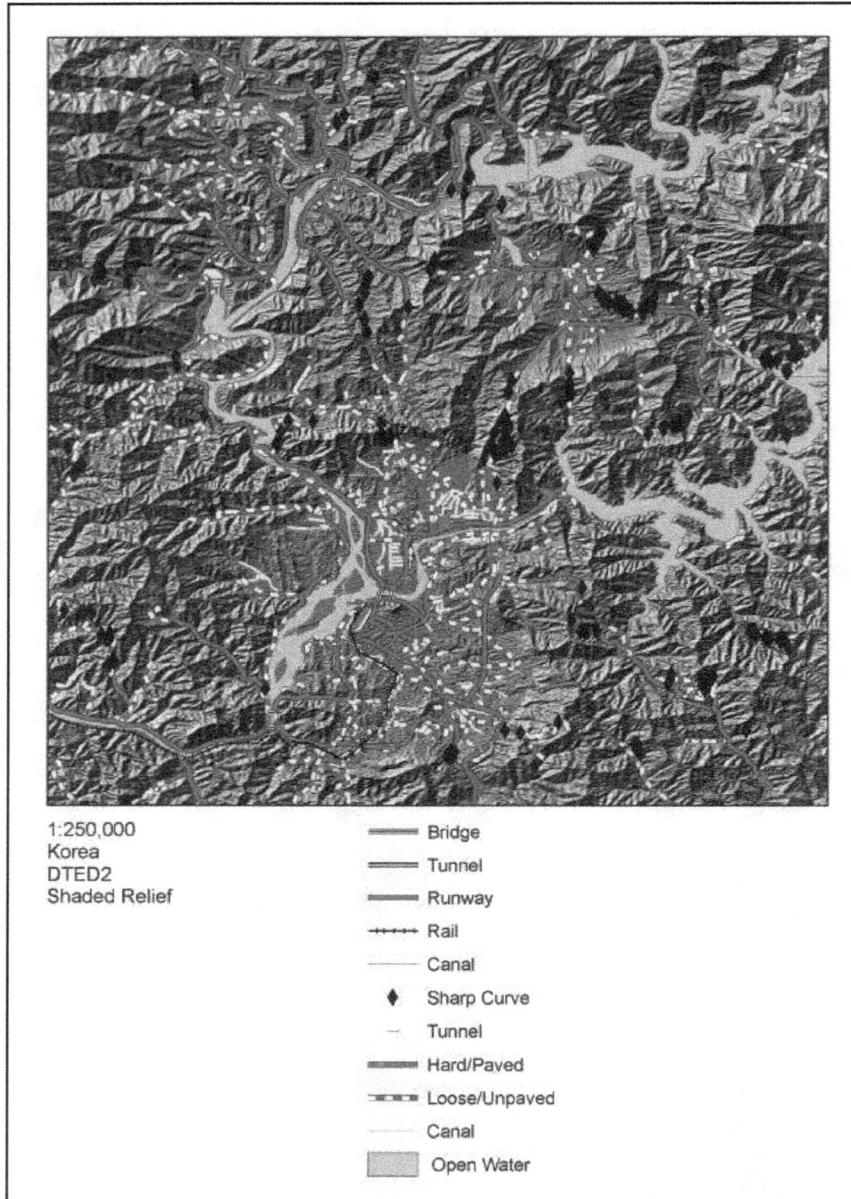

Figure A-7. Example of a product showing LOCs

# HYDROLOGY ANALYSIS

A-12. Hydrology overlays (see figure A-8) identify drainage features by size and location. Where interim terrain data (ITD)/vector interim terrain data (VITD) (or other detailed vector data) exist, geospatial engineers can provide a wide variety of detail about drainage features, such as widths, depths, water velocity, bank heights, vegetation along banks, and bottom materials. These data can also include areas influenced by tidal fluctuations. These overlays may be used to evaluate friendly and enemy COAs and highlight conditions that can impose a major operational or logistical concern.

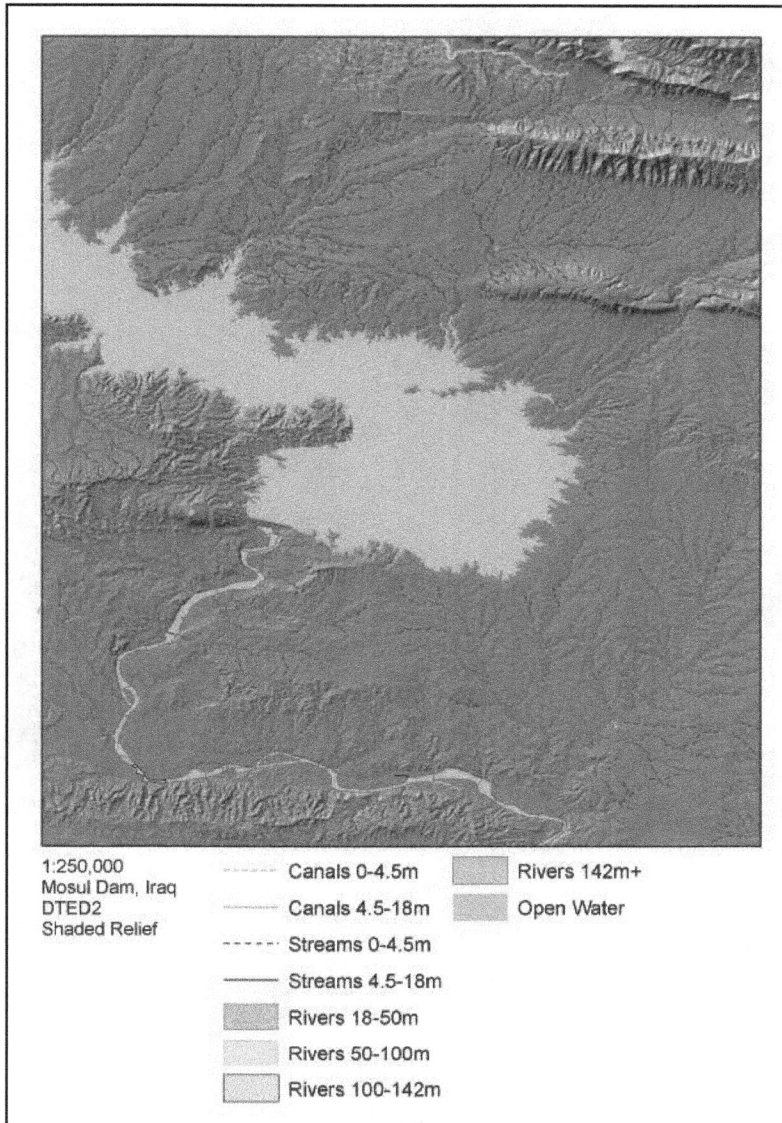

1:250,000
Mosul Dam, Iraq
DTED2
Shaded Relief

- - - - - Canals 0-4.5m
~~~~~~~ Canals 4.5-18m
- - - - - Streams 0-4.5m
———— Streams 4.5-18m
Rivers 18-50m
Rivers 50-100m
Rivers 100-142m
Rivers 142m+
Open Water

**Figure A-8. Example of a hydrology overlay**

## DROP ZONES

A-13. This product (see figure A-9) helps planners quickly template possible drop zones in support of airborne operations. Drop zone overlays use slope (less than 10 percent slope for personnel and less than 30 percent slope for equipment) as the limiting factor. In addition to slope, cover and concealment and accessibility (entry and exit routes) must also be considered.

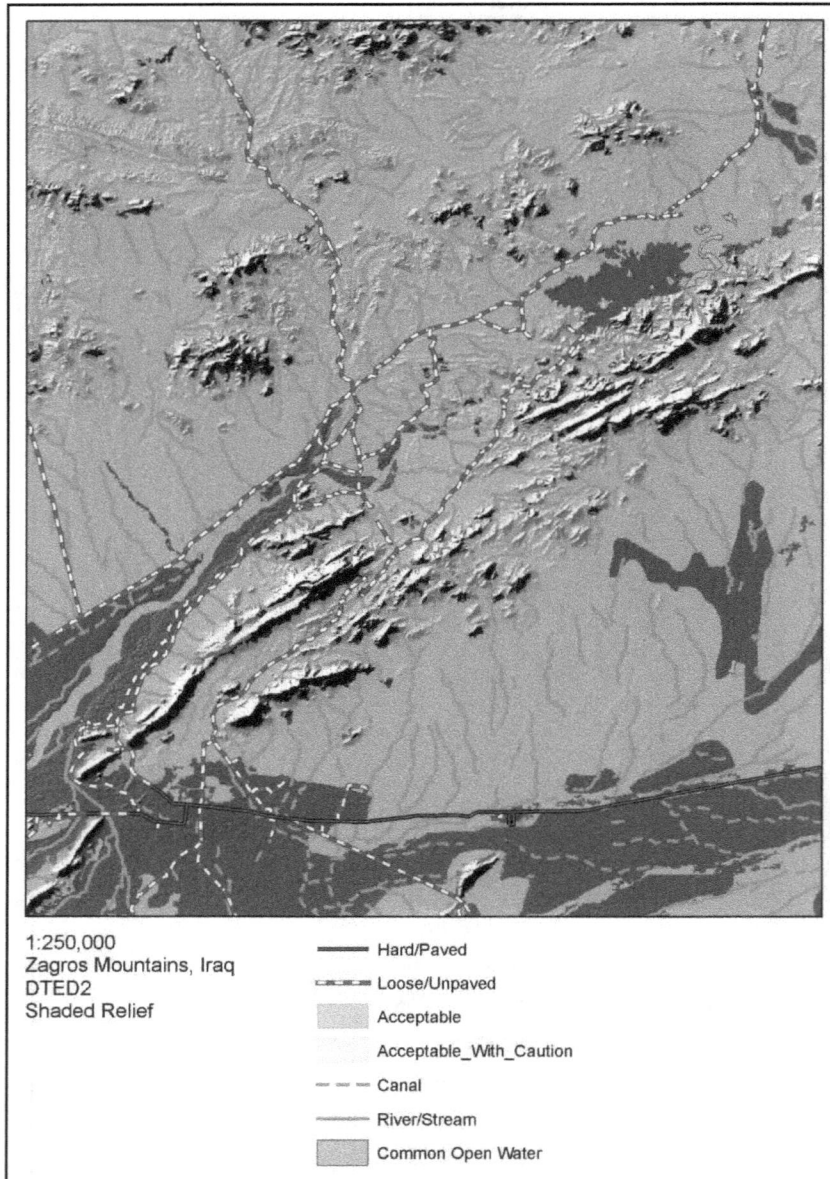

Figure A-9. Example of a product showing potential drop zones

## HELICOPTER LANDING ZONES

A-14. This product helps planners quickly template possible landing zones in support of air assault operations. Helicopter landing zone overlays (see figure A-10) depict suitable open areas (no trees) that have less than 15 percent slope. Soil conditions should also be evaluated to avoid areas that may contribute to brown-out conditions for pilots.

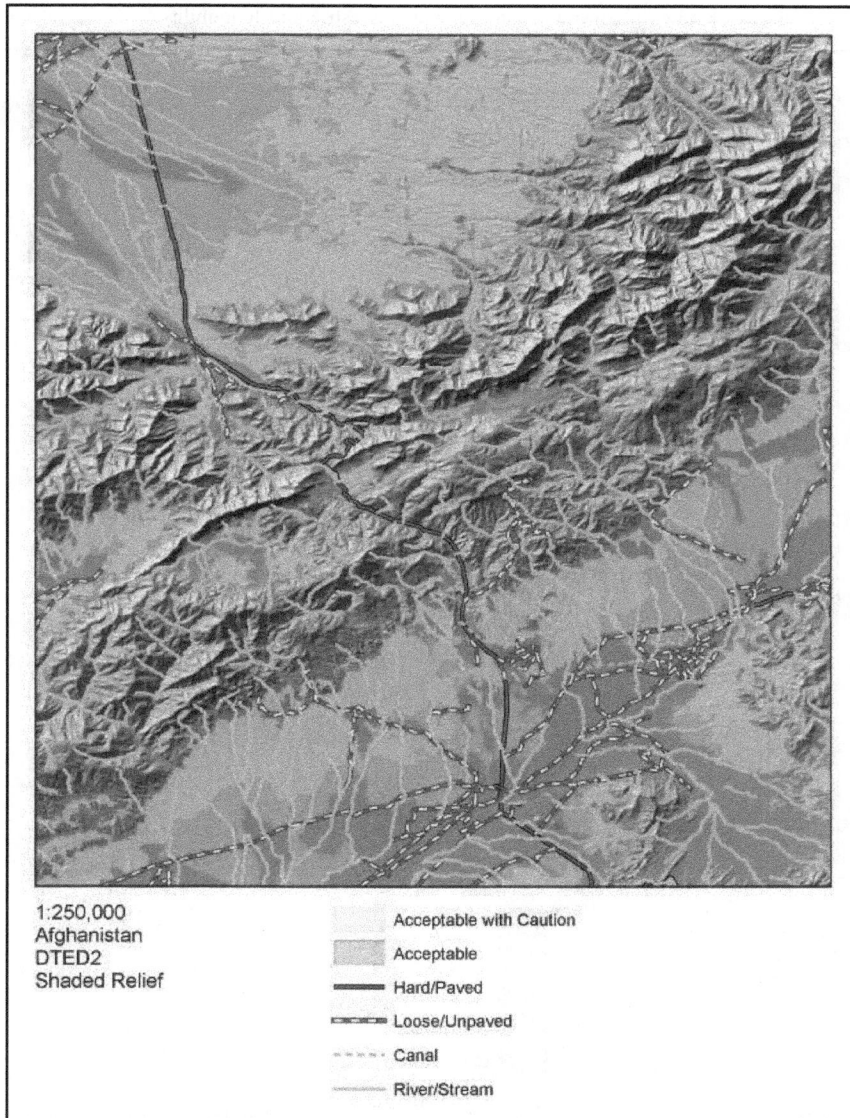

1:250,000
Afghanistan
DTED2
Shaded Relief

Acceptable with Caution
Acceptable
Hard/Paved
Loose/Unpaved
Canal
River/Stream

**Figure A-10. Example of a product showing potential helicopter landing zones**

## VEGETATION ANALYSIS

A-15. This product (see figure A-11) shows the effects of vegetation in an operational area, based on the types of trees (coniferous, deciduous, or mixed), tree heights, stem diameter, stem spacing, and canopy closures. It also reflects information about cultivated areas, such as types of crops (wet or dry) and whether the area is terraced or not. This product can help planners determine the suitability of an area based primarily on the availability of cover and concealment and restrictions to mobility.

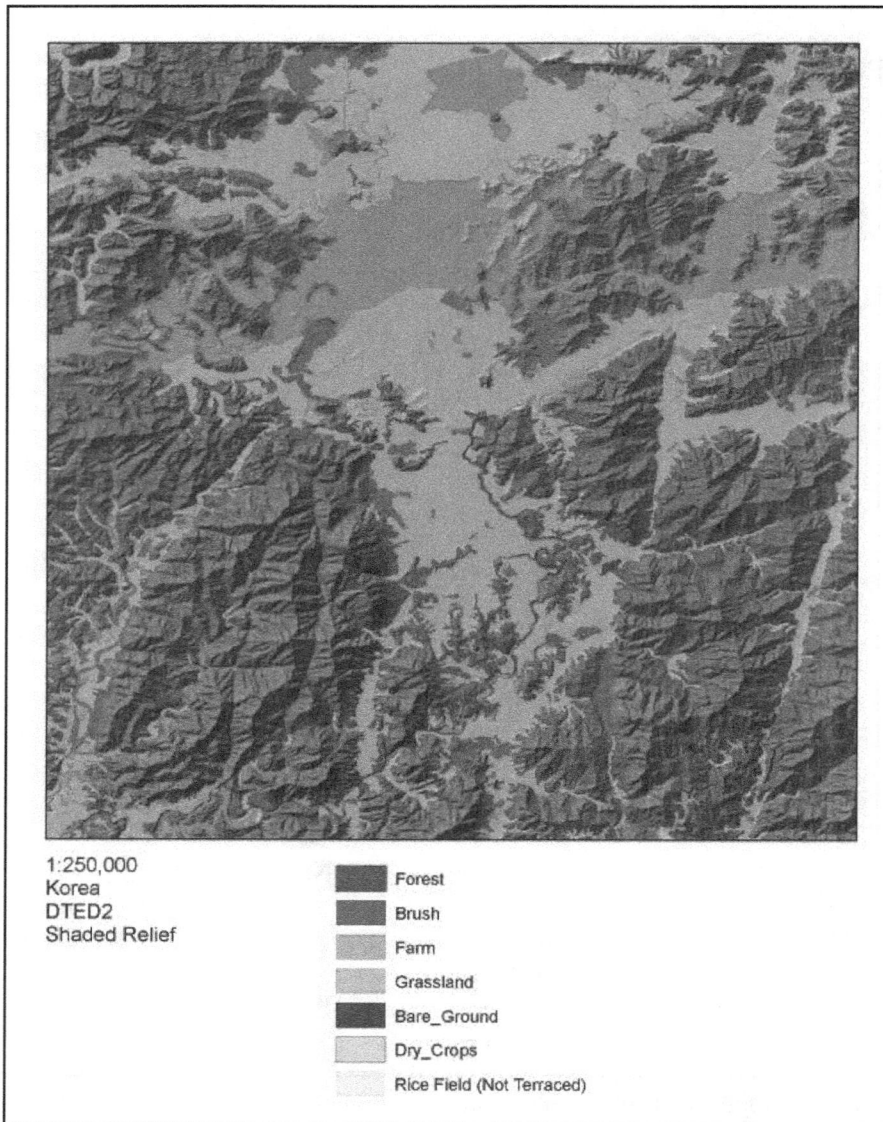

Figure A-11. Example of a product showing the effects of vegetation

## SOIL TRAFFICABILITY

A-16. This product (see figure A-12) shows the effects of soil on trafficability, usually based on the type of soil and its moisture content. Fine-grained soils (such as silt and clay) and highly organic soils (referred to as peat) severely restrict or prohibit movement, while dry and compact soils are more trafficable.

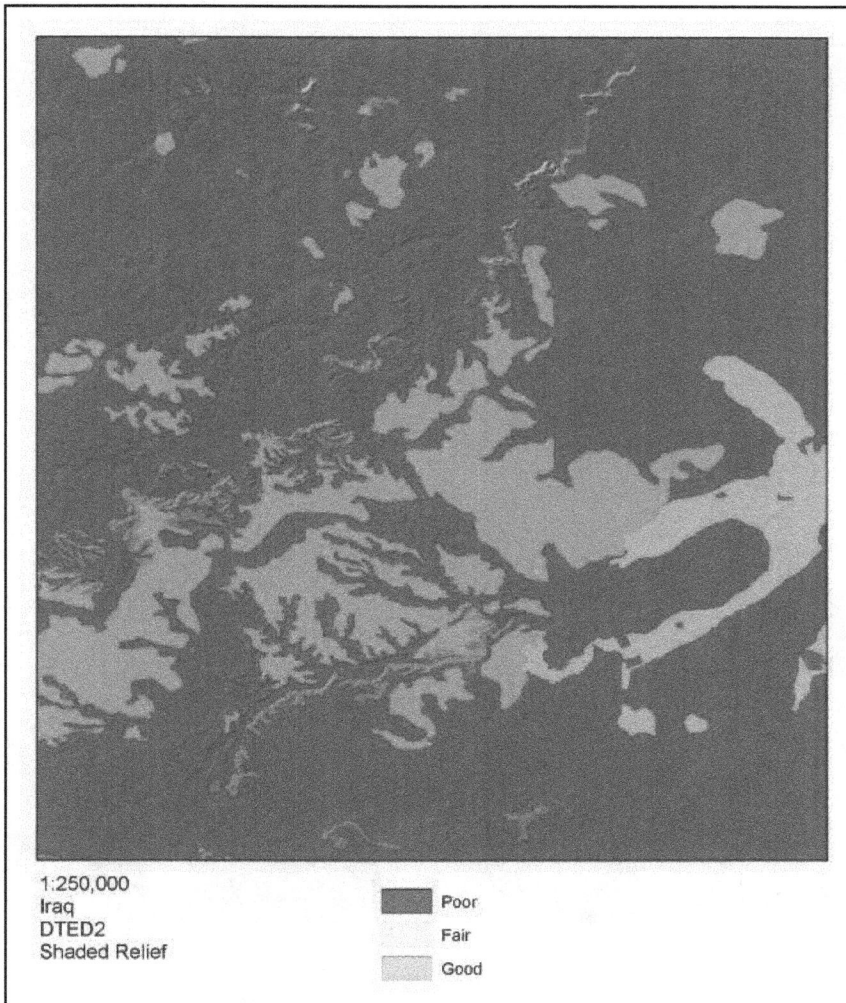

1:250,000
Iraq
DTED2
Shaded Relief

Poor
Fair
Good

**Figure A-12. Example of a product showing the effects of soil on trafficability**

## FIELD OF FIRE

A-17. A field-of-fire product (see figure A-13) shows the area that can be effectively covered from a specific position based on LOS and weapon capabilities. This product is used to locate defensible terrain, identify potential EAs, and position fighting systems to allow mutually supporting fires. It can also reveal where maneuvering forces are more vulnerable to ambush.

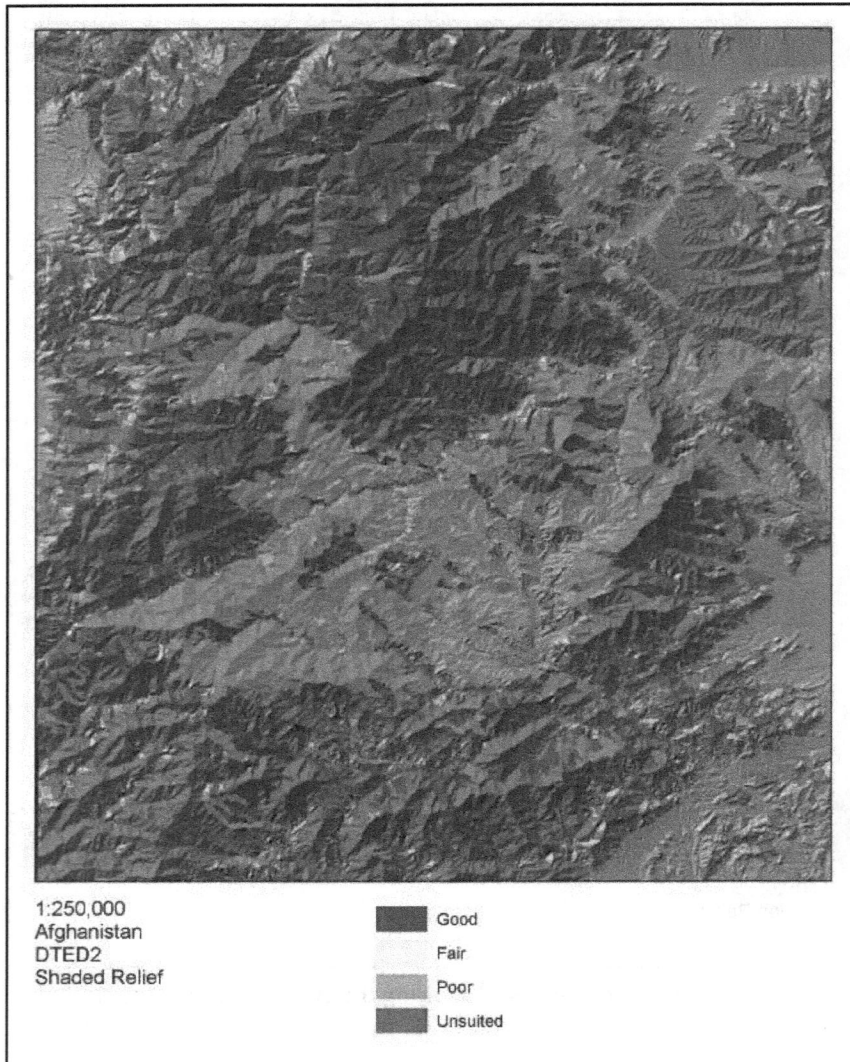

1:250,000
Afghanistan
DTED2
Shaded Relief

Good
Fair
Poor
Unsuited

**Figure A-13. Example of a product showing fields of fire**

## ARTILLERY SLOPE TINT

A-18. This product (see figure A-14) depicts AIs for artillery assets where slope is the primary limiting factor. Areas with a slope from 0 to 7 percent are considered suitable for artillery firing positions, while 8 to 12 percent slope is considered marginal. This product helps template enemy artillery assets by narrowing down the likely areas for firing positions based on slope restrictions.

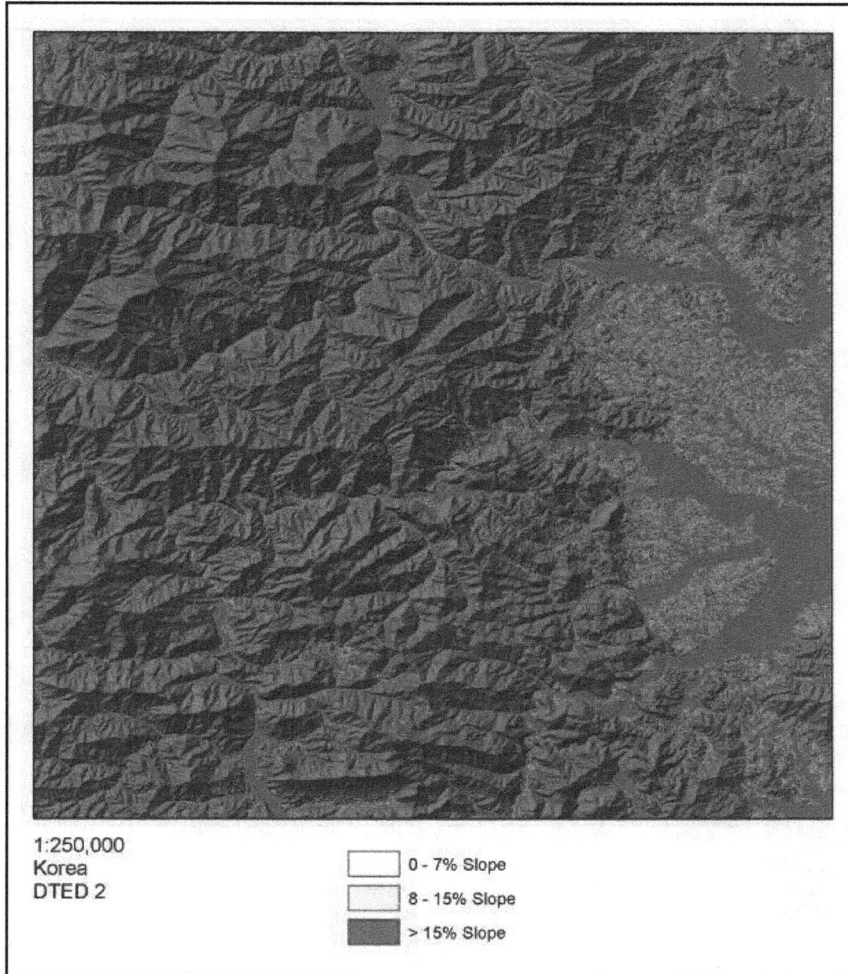

1:250,000
Korea
DTED 2

☐ 0 - 7% Slope
☐ 8 - 15% Slope
■ > 15% Slope

**Figure A-14. Example of a product showing artillery slope tint**

## AERIAL CONCEALMENT

A-19. The aerial concealment overlay (see figure A-15) shows the most suitable areas to conceal a force from overhead detection, based on the analysis of woods, underbrush, tall grass, and cultivated vegetation. This product is predicated on canopy closure information within the vegetation layer. This overlay is particularly useful in templating areas where unconventional enemy forces may be operating. It can also help friendly forces identify concealed movement routes and staging areas.

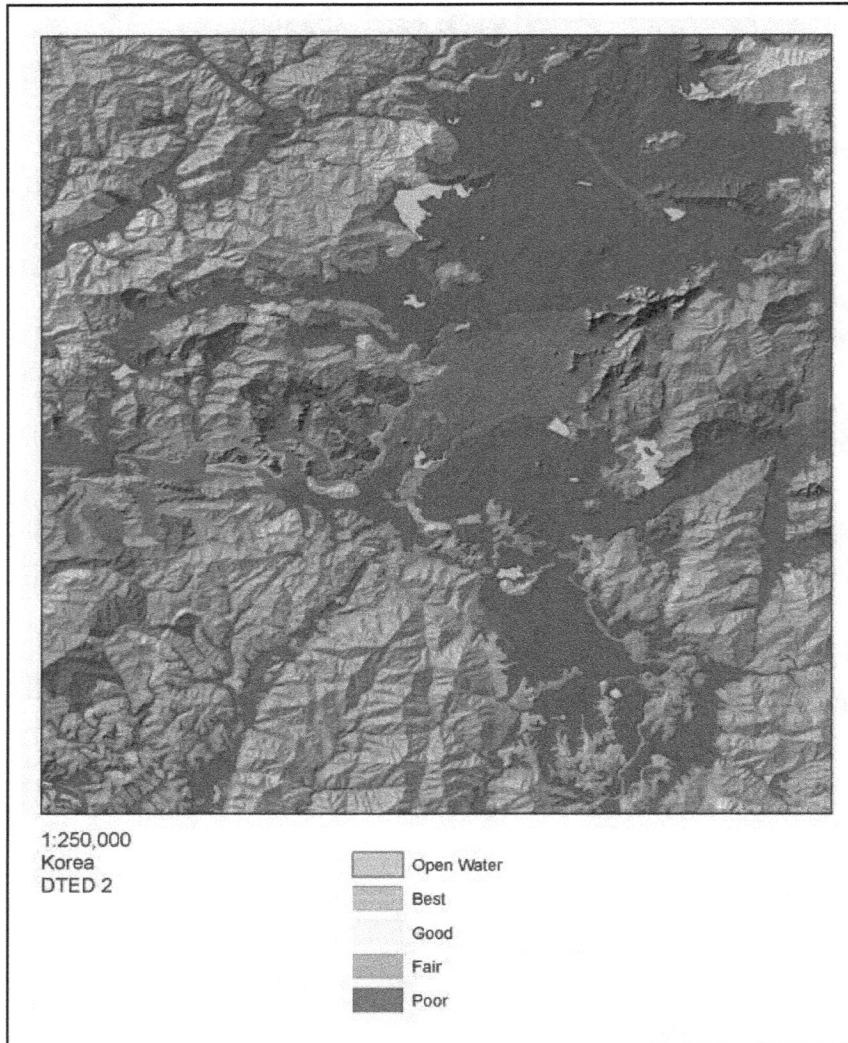

1:250,000
Korea
DTED 2

Open Water
Best
Good
Fair
Poor

**Figure A-15. Example of a product showing aerial concealment**

## SURFACE MATERIAL

A-20. The surface material overlay (see figure A-16) shows a contrast based on the predominant type of soil that constitutes an area's surface. This information is useful in determining the trafficability of an area, assessing the ease of excavating fighting positions, and planning construction projects that are better suited on certain types of soil.

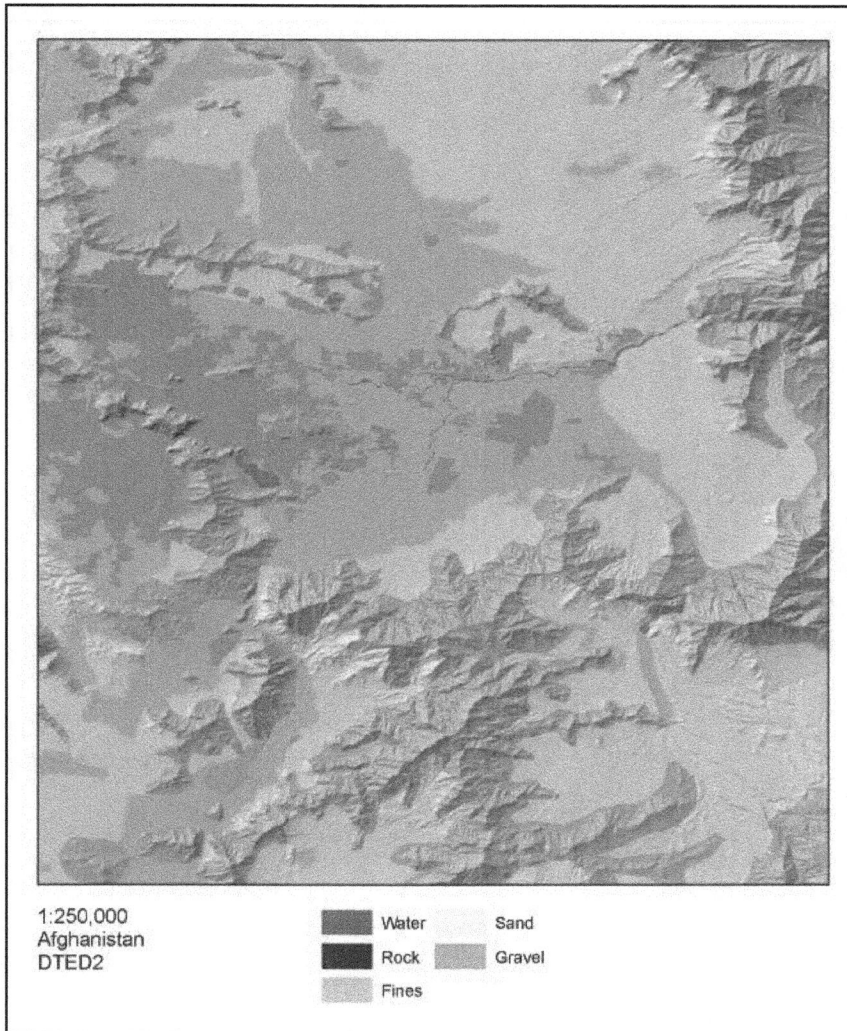

1:250,000
Afghanistan
DTED2

Water    Sand
Rock    Gravel
Fines

**Figure A-16. Example of a surface material overlay**

## CONSTRUCTION RESOURCES

A-21. This product (see figure A-17) shows the natural construction resources of an area. This product can help engineers plan major construction projects (such as roads and base camps) that are benefitted by having close access to certain types of construction materials that can be made readily available through quarrying.

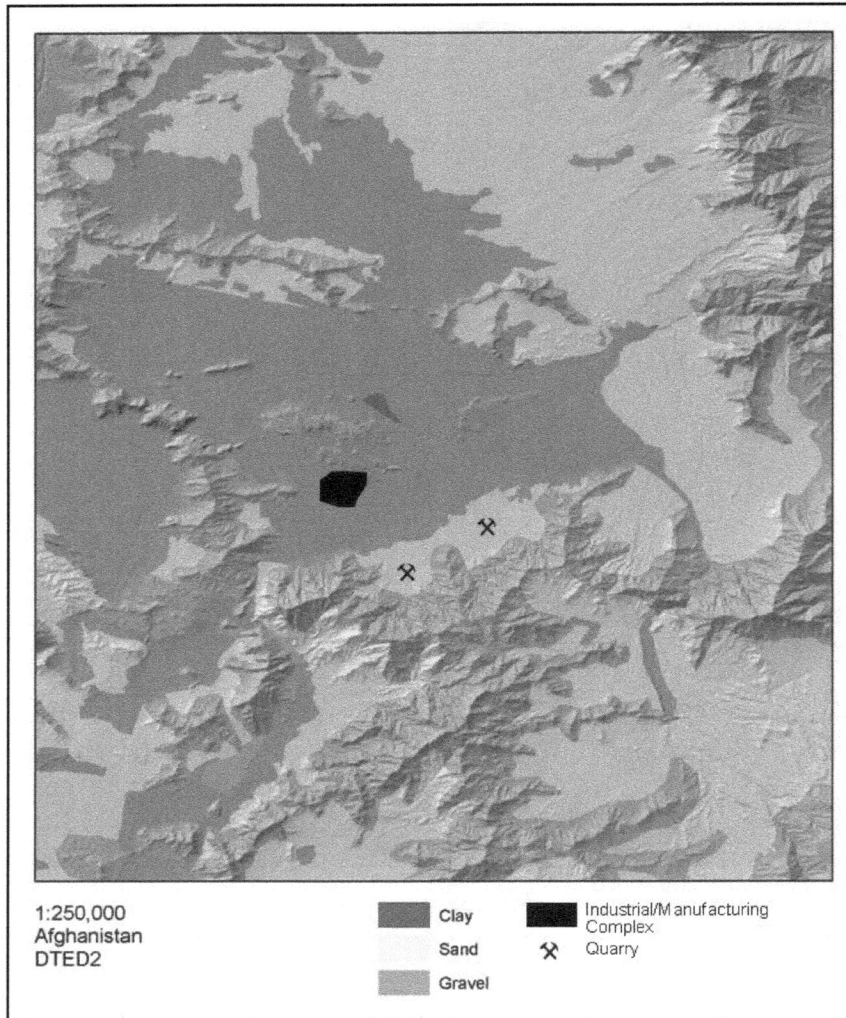

1:250,000
Afghanistan
DTED2

Clay
Sand
Gravel
Industrial/Manufacturing Complex
Quarry

**Figure A-17. Example of a product showing construction resources**

## SHADED RELIEF

A-22. A shaded relief image (see figure A-18) creates the illusion of a 3-D view of an area by mimicking shadows of the sun to highlight variations in elevation and slope. This product can be depicted in gray scale or a single-color range, or it can be color-coded to enhance its appearance.

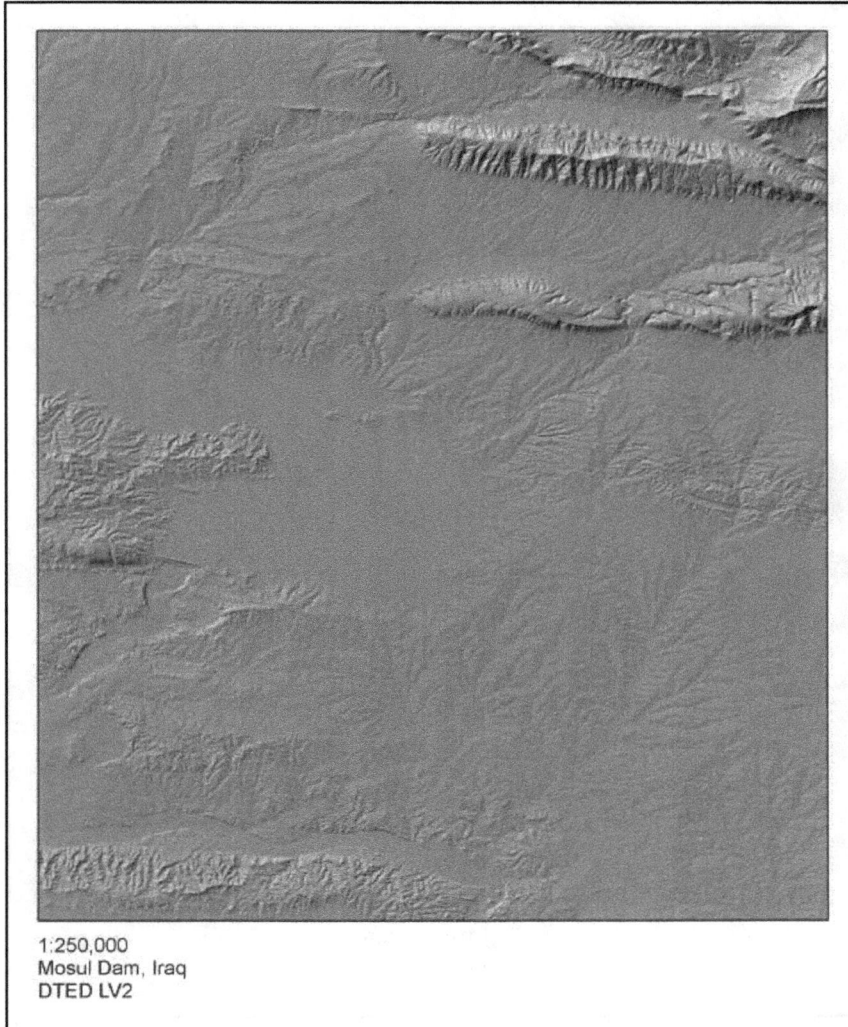

1:250,000
Mosul Dam, Iraq
DTED LV2

**Figure A-18. Example of a shaded relief image**

## LOS ANALYSIS

A-23. LOS profiles (see figure A-19) show an area of direct observation that is possible from one location to another based on DTED. LOS analysis is used in templating enemy positions, positioning friendly capabilities (such as LOS-based communications and observation platforms), and developing EAs. The accuracy of this analysis is directly proportional to the level of DTED available.

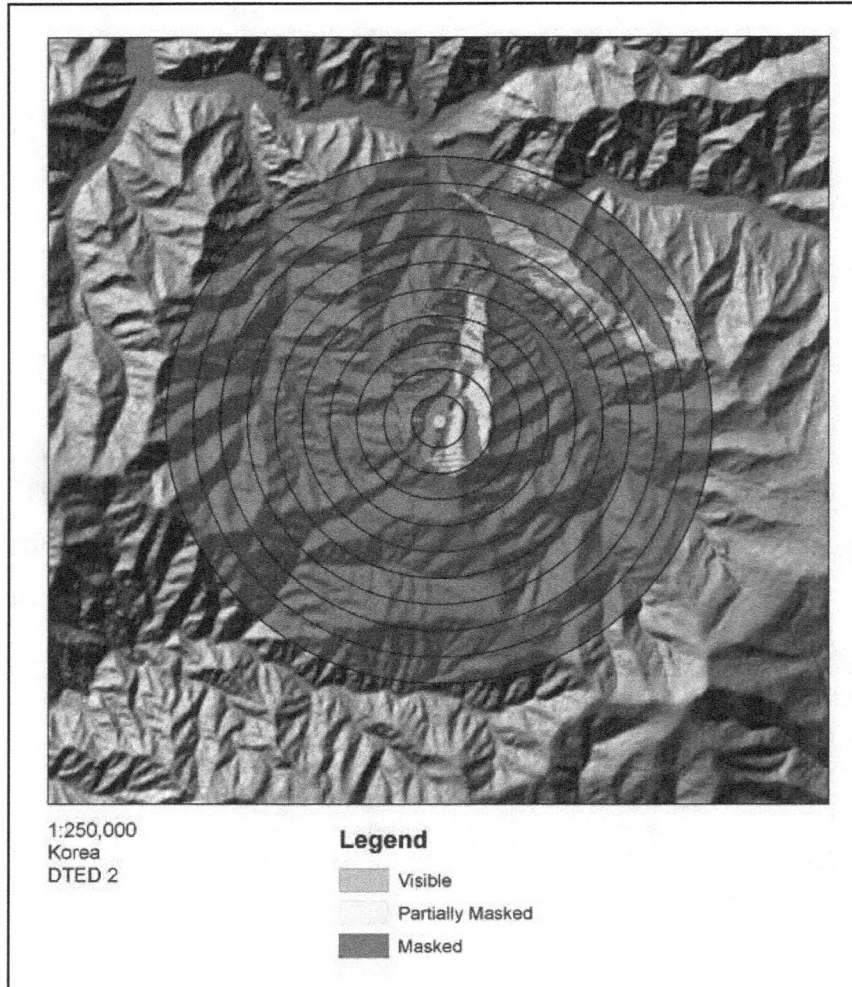

1:250,000
Korea
DTED 2

**Legend**

Visible

Partially Masked

Masked

**Figure A-19. Example of an LOS profile**

## PERSPECTIVE VIEW

A-24. This product (see figure A-20) is a 3-D visual depiction of an area from an observer's point of view that is produced by combining imagery layers with elevation data. The display can include roads, rivers, operational graphics, and text to enhance the visualization of the terrain.

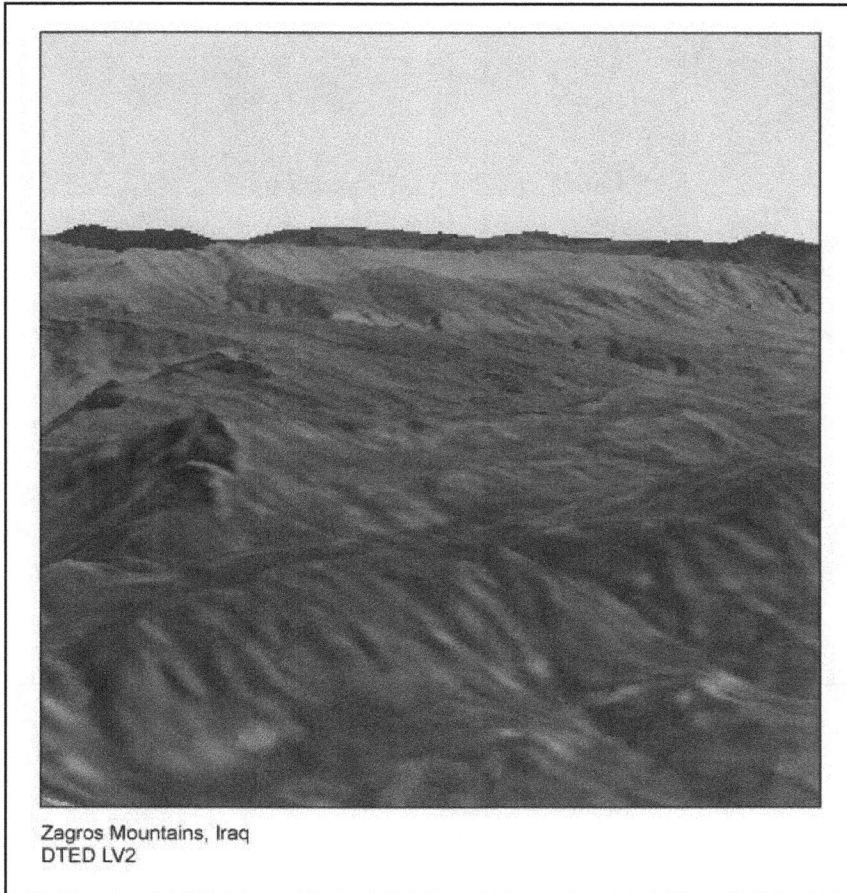

Zagros Mountains, Iraq
DTED LV2

**Figure A-20. Example of a perspective view**

## FLY-THROUGH

A-25. This product (see figure A-21) is a computer-generated view of an area along a specified flight line at a specified altitude and angle viewed from inside the aircraft. The display can include roads, rivers, operational graphics, and text to enhance the visualization of the terrain.

Figure A-21. Example of a product showing a fly-through

## URBAN TACTICAL PLANNER

A-26. The Urban Tactical Planner™ (UTP) (see figure A-22) is an interactive fly-through application that is similar to Google Earth™; it displays key aspects of the urban area in thematic layers that are overlaid on high-resolution imagery or maps. UTP provides an overview of the urban terrain in the form of maps, imagery, elevation data, perspective views, handheld photography, video clips, and building information. Geospatial engineer teams have the capability of incorporating new data and imagery into UTP and placing it on a digital video disc in UTP format for distribution in the field.

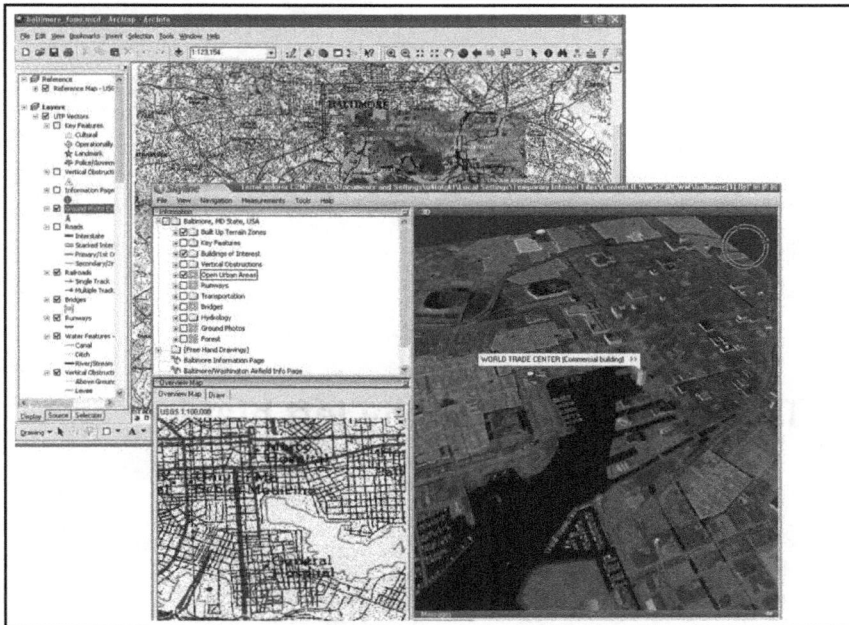

**Figure A-22. Example of a UTP product**

This page intentionally left blank.

# Geospatial Data Management

The Army capitalizes on the information-sharing capabilities enabled by the ABCS to facilitate decisionmaking. To be effective, ABCS relies on access to current, accurate, and common geospatial data residing in shared, distributed geospatial databases to form the foundation of the COP. The unique nature of geospatial data—their size and diversity—presents management challenges. Geospatial data differ from other data in that they contain structured data (location, shape, and orientation) about objects in relation to the earth's surface—making the data extremely large and cumbersome. They also originate from various sensors, national resources, intelligence assets, HN resources, and reconnaissance forces in a variety of formats that increase the potential for inconsistencies. Geospatial engineers are charged with managing these data through an enterprise geospatial database that aims at allowing multiple applications to simultaneously use the same geospatial data for different purposes at different echelons. This appendix discusses those requirements and provides considerations for effectively managing geospatial databases in support of full spectrum operations.

## DIGITAL GEOSPATIAL DATA

B-1. Geospatial data must be disseminated to the ABCS as rapidly as possible while ensuring their security and retaining their integrity. Figure B-1, page B-2, shows how geospatial engineers will integrate within the Distributed Common Ground System–Army (DCGS–A) architecture, based on the migration of DTSS into DCGS–A. This concept is based on the transition of DTSS to a service-oriented architecture that will allow geospatial engineers to better serve their customers and gain access to information stored throughout the battle command network.

B-2. The two types of services (product and discovery) are enabled through metadata (data about data) that will reside on a metadata catalog. This requires data or products posted on a server to be accompanied with appropriate metadata, which will allow users to search for products or data, as well as obtain services. Metadata allows discovery services in two ways. The first is a simple search feature that allows users to search key phrases, dates, AI, names, product and data types, and so forth. The second allows geospatial engineers and other analysts to set up alerts that are triggered when a product or data that meet their predefined query are posted on the network. This allows data, once posted, to find the analyst instead of the analyst having to search for them.

B-3. Services will provide the staff with faster access to geospatial products. Some of the more common geospatial products (such as LOS, CCM, and helicopter landing zone) can be provided through Web services, in which a customer accesses the Web using a thin-client approach to submit product requests. With certain situations, customers can actually create their own products by entering a few key parameters.

B-4. Orchestrating this effort begins with an understanding of the desired end state based on the data user's requirements. This includes requirements for geospatial data storage, manipulation (the ability to process updates), and multidimensional displays. Geospatial engineers then determine what data sets are being developed by national agencies and how they will be distributed to users, including the dissemination of GI generated by theater-level geospatial capabilities and the reverse flow of enhanced geospatial data that will update national databases.

B-5. All geospatial data users must adhere to the established enterprise geospatial database requirements for using digital geospatial data in the mapping tool kits in the ABCS and GI&S software applications. Based on the digital terrain data, mapping tool kit operators can evaluate the operational area or specific AO, develop a limited set of TDAs, and provide an accurate digital display of the digital terrain data.

B-6. The digital terrain data's framework will be implemented in stages varying in resolution and area coverage. The framework consists of—

- NGA data.
- TGD.
- Field collected/generated data.

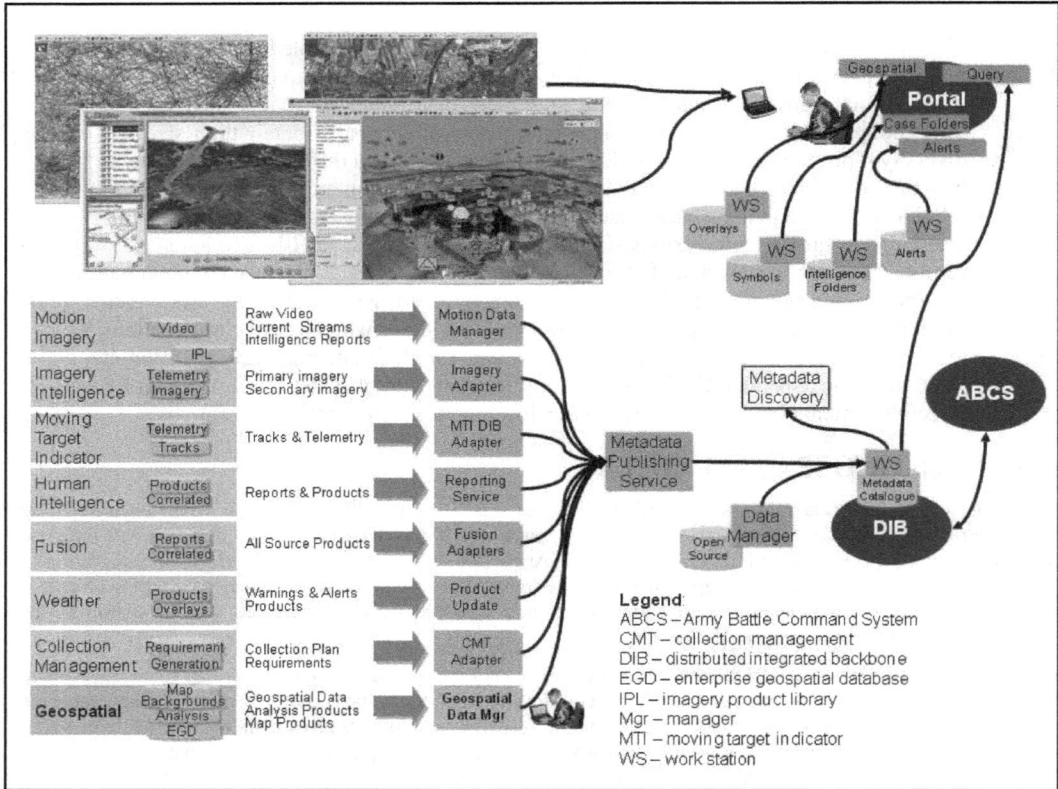

**Figure B-1. Geospatial data flow and fusion in DCGS–A**

## NATIONAL GEOSPATIAL–INTELLIGENCE AGENCY DATA

B-7. NGA provides the data that form the foundation terrain data sets initially used by all Army units before deployment. Based on preexisting data prepared from national sources for dissemination to all military users, the data consist of elevation, feature, and imagery data and are typically incomplete, out of date, or in many cases nonexistent (such as with Grenada, the Balkans, and Afghanistan). NGA provides the data electronically through their Non-Secure Internet Protocol Router Network (NIPRNET), SIPRNET, and Joint Worldwide Intelligence Communications System gateways and in hard copy through the DLA and the Army supply system.

## THEATER GEOSPATIAL DATABASE

B-8. NGA data form the foundation of the TGD that each GPC manages for its assigned theater of operations. As the central authority for all geospatial data in the theater, the GPC ensures the distribution of geospatial data to all geospatial units at each echelon. The GPC also collects enriched data from those units and evaluates, corrects, updates, and incorporates it into the TGD and provides updated data to the NGA for inclusion in its national geospatial databases.

## FIELD-COLLECTED/GENERATED DATA

B-9. Field-collected/generated data are the data generated to update the geospatial databases residing at the national level down to the BCT. The generation of enriched data relies on both top-down and bottom-up feeds. While top-down feeds can result from multiple sources, bottom-up feeds primarily rely on the result of ISR operations at the tactical level using systems such as—

- Air and ground reconnaissance (including engineer survey teams).
- Unmanned aircraft systems.
- IMINT or HUMINT sources.

B-10. Data retrieved from tactical units are normally provided through digital and voice reports or imagery to the tactical operations center. Issues regarding the validity of the data are normally addressed by the senior geospatial engineer, while concerns about the quality of the data rest with the intelligence staff. After all issues pertaining to the validity or quality of the data are resolved, the database manager updates the master database according to established procedures or SOP and passes the updated data to the geospatial engineer team at higher headquarters. The enrichment data provided by subordinate units are then consolidated and organized to enable an enterprise geospatial database at that echelon. For example, reports from BCT to division showing individual minefields are consolidated with terrain data. The information is then presented on a COO that shows a more comprehensive picture of the mobility restrictions in the division's AO.

# ENTERPRISE GEOSPATIAL DATABASE DEVELOPMENT

B-11. Geospatial database development and maintenance is a continuous process and a shared responsibility by geospatial engineers at each echelon down to BCT. The data management sections in the GPCs are responsible for the development and maintenance of the TGD and help the topographic companies and geospatial engineer teams in acquiring data and building their respective databases. Figure B-2 shows the primary functions and supporting tasks performed by the GPC in managing the TGD in relation to the four major functions of geospatial engineering.

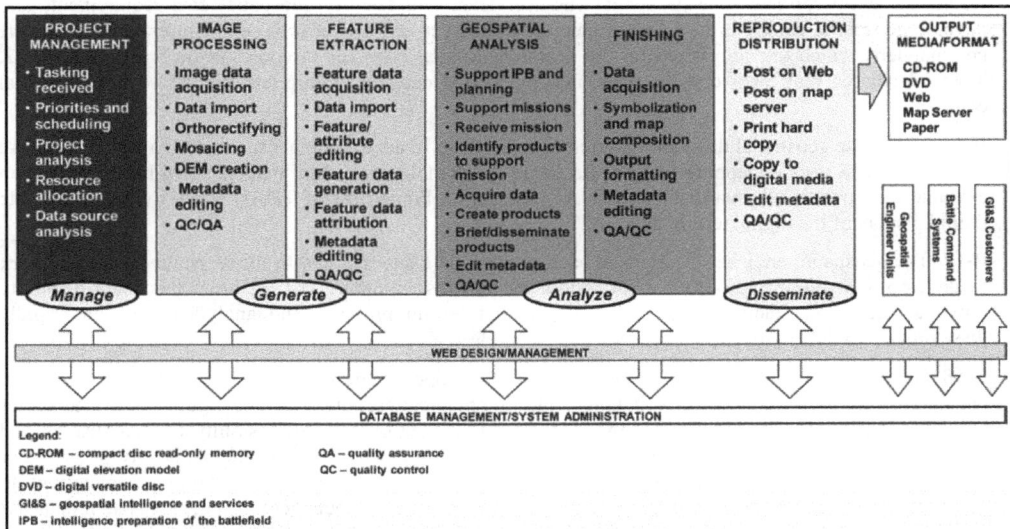

Figure B-2. Primary functions of the GPC in managing the TGD

B-12. The majority of geospatial database development occurs in anticipation of future operations before deployment. In cooperation with higher headquarters, geospatial engineers monitor the status of geospatial data covering their AORs. These data are normally provided to the GPC by the NGA, the AGC, and other national sources. Geospatial engineers use the available geospatial data to develop initial databases that serve as the basic reference for the production of GI in support of the operational commander's planning requirements. In preparation for deployment, geospatial engineer units acquire and load geospatial data provided by the GPC into primary and secondary servers containing the master databases. Once deployed, the geospatial engineer team's data-management element manages the secondary map file server and maintains the supported unit's geospatial data and terrain products. This includes the digital maps used by the unit's ABCS, which enable ABCS operators to evaluate the terrain using the embedded mapping tool kit. Deployed geospatial engineer units maintain configuration-management control over the digital geospatial data for their supported unit.

B-13. Following deployment, field-collected/generated data will be gathered using all means available to facilitate the creation of geospatial products in support of IPB and other integrating processes. Close coordination and working interfaces should be established with the intelligence staff to ensure access and acquisition of imagery data through national imagery and other intelligence data sources early in the operation.

B-14. Distributing in-theater updates and data feeds to echelons below BCT can be the most challenging aspect of geospatial data dissemination. This involves moving data from higher to lower and from dispersed and possibly engaged forces to the nearest geospatial engineer element, which may not have a terrain-data file server. The geospatial engineer team organic to the BCT establishes and manages the enterprise geospatial database. Updates to this initial database are disseminated through established tactical networks or removable media devices as prescribed in mission orders or SOPs. These updates typically require less memory than the full enterprise geospatial database, since the ABCS is normally provided with an initial load before deployment. Tactical updates and feedback resulting from operations at the lower tactical levels are submitted to higher headquarters (and eventually to the NGA) using the method that was used for disseminating products, but in reverse. The provision of tactical updates and feedback is critical in establishing the most accurate geospatial data for other users.

B-15. The ENCOORD, S-2/G-2, S-3/G-3, and the geospatial engineers and imagery analysts in the GEOINT cell work during the planning phase to fulfill GI requirements through ISR collection, RFIs, and reachback as appropriate. The geospatial engineer team will identify geospatial data requirements and develop geospatial databases using the requirements cited by the operational commander and subordinate commanders, which are prioritized by the senior geospatial engineer in coordination with the S-2/G-2. These databases may also contain other information as deemed appropriate by the senior geospatial engineer.

B-16. Enterprise geospatial database requirements are established at the highest echelon to ensure database integrity. ABCS uses a mapping tool kit. Based on the digital terrain data, mapping tool kit operators can evaluate the operational area or a specific AO, develop a limited set of TDAs, and provide an accurate digital display of the digital terrain data.

B-17. The geospatial engineer elements at each echelon, in cooperation with the respective S-2/G-2, work to develop and rehearse procedures for producing and disseminating GI. Enabling this interoperability down to the lowest tactical level helps ensure that terrain products and analytical data are rapidly disseminated to the appropriate data users.

B-18. Geospatial data are exchanged among the GPCs, topographic engineer companies, and geospatial engineering teams at the various echelons using communication networks (see figure B-3). The senior geospatial engineer at each echelon down to the BCT has the overall responsibility for establishing and standardizing the procedures for populating the database within the respective echelon. Newly generated or obtained geospatial data are checked, validated, and cataloged using uniform naming conventions to facilitate the use of the database. This provides ABCS users with efficient access to the geospatial database residing on the DTSS and Maneuver Control System servers.

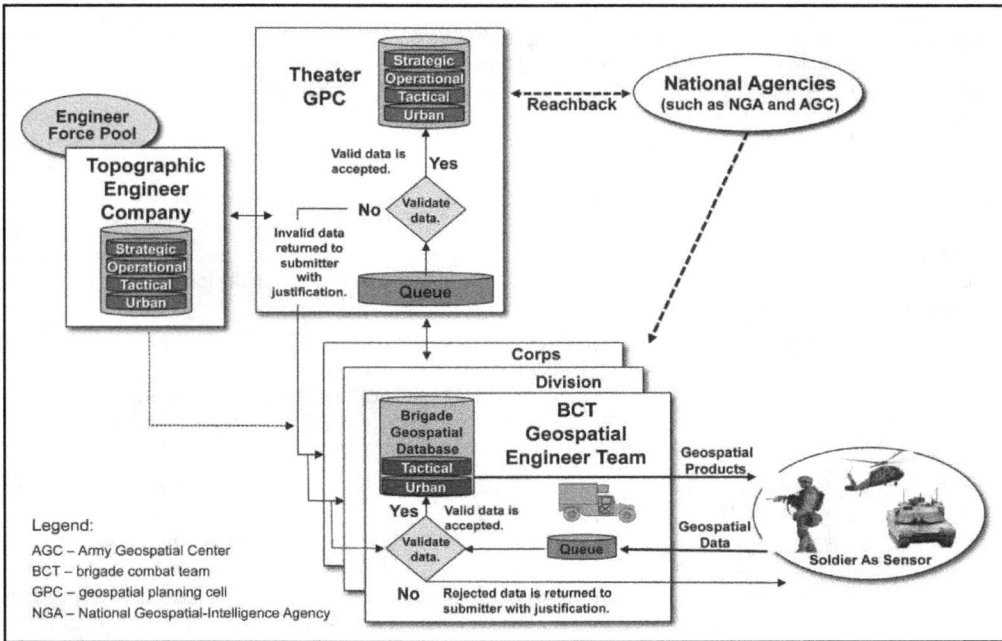

**Figure B-3. Enterprise geospatial data flow**

B-19. The senior geospatial engineer, in coordination with the S-2/G-2 and the S-3/G-3, oversees the data-management element located in the main CP. The noncommissioned officer in charge (NCOIC) of the data-management element manages the terrain-data file server and oversees and directs the terrain analysts in populating, updating, and archiving geospatial databases. The NCOIC helps in developing standardized procedures and enforcing policies related to filing, formatting, storing, retrieving, and archiving the geospatial data acquired for all geospatial engineer elements within the command. The NCOIC also coordinates with the division G-2 to establish dissemination priorities for topographical folders or products based on division and BCT requirements. The senior geospatial engineer at the BCT main CP follows the established procedures in managing the BCT database in coordination with the BCT S-2.

B-20. When operating in a multinational environment, the geospatial engineering team must work closely with the ENCOORD and S-2/G-2 at various echelons to develop procedures for disseminating GI updates to those mission partners without access to digital battle command systems to ensure data integrity throughout the command.

B-21. A database management system (DBMS) is computer software designed to manage databases that control the organization, storage, and retrieval of data. The DBMS embedded in the DTSS helps the geospatial engineer manage geospatial data. The DBMS automatically correlates data from various sources, enabling the analyst to manipulate the data to create and disseminate new or updated geospatial products. The DBMS also facilitates the exchange or addition of new categories of data, such as digital maps or overlays, without major disruptions to ongoing work.

B-22. The GPC is a critical node in the overall geospatial enterprise architecture. Each GPC is responsible for data generation and quality control of data in its operational area. This provides a single point of responsibility and increases the confidence level of geospatial data within a theater and prevents duplication of effort that can result in multiple, conflicting data sets. The desired end state is to have every GPC's TGD data mirrored at a central location for Armywide access (such as the AGC), and to have those data accepted and included in NGA's national database.

B-23. GPCs must coordinate with each other and develop coproduction agreements to reduce duplication of effort and facilitate the management of geospatial data-generation and -collection activities in their respective operational areas. Each GPC will generally only maintain data that are required for its operational area—a TGD does not need to mirror every other TGD. In special situations where a GPC may need to access data residing in another GPC's operational area, it can subscribe to updates based on metadata, such as the country code and the operational level of the data (strategic, operational, tactical, or urban). If a GPC enters into a coproduction agreement with another TGD, the validation and acceptance of data belongs with the TGD responsible for that theater.

B-24. The GPC may be augmented with NGA geospatial analysts, cartographic analysts, and data stewards to greatly enhance its ability to manage the TGD and ensure the quality of data generated by the GPC and subordinates in meeting national mapping accuracy standards for subsequent inclusion and redistribution in NGA's national and regional databases.

B-25. All geospatial data within an area must be cross-referenced to ensure accuracy and that they provide the same terrain information through varying levels of scale. Geospatial engineers compare scales and metadata associated with the data to identify any inconsistencies, and modify the appropriate levels as needed. Any changes to verified NGA data (such as vector map [VMAP] and feature foundation data) will be reported to NGA and to the other GPCs to ensure database consistency.

B-26. TGD features are stored in a geospatial database and organized in four levels of resolution or scales which are shown in figure B-4. These four levels are—

- **Strategic level**. Generally equivalent to 1:1,000,000 scales and have features associated with standard NGA maps at this scale (such as NGA VMAP level 0).
- **Operational level**. Generally equivalent to 1:250,000 scale. Newly extracted data must adhere to NGA cartographic standards at this map scale (such as NGA VMAP level 1, feature foundation data, and planning ITD).
- **Tactical level**. Generally equivalent to 1:50,000 scale, but can range from 1:100,000 to 1:10,000 scale (such as NGA VMAP level 2 and VITD and ITD).
- **Urban level**. Any special products that are 1:10,000 or larger, such as NGA urban VMAP or the AGC's urban tactical planning data.

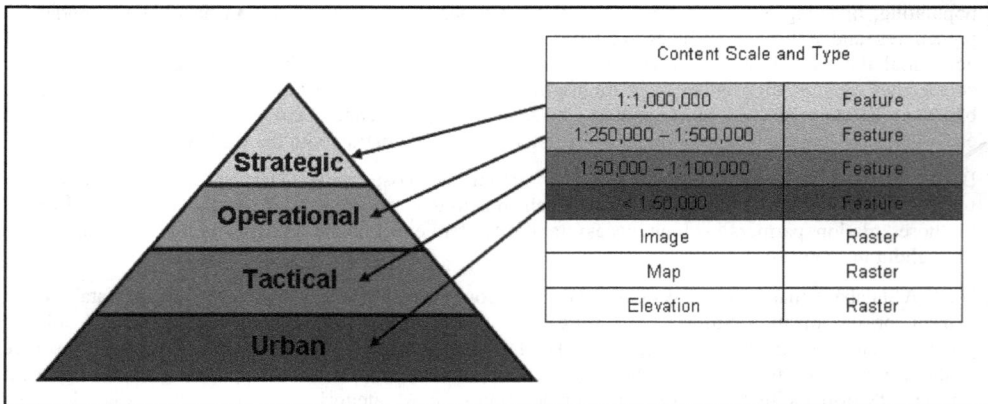

| Content Scale and Type | |
| --- | --- |
| 1:1,000,000 | Feature |
| 1:250,000 – 1:500,000 | Feature |
| 1:50,000 – 1:100,000 | Feature |
| < 1:50,000 | Feature |
| Image | Raster |
| Map | Raster |
| Elevation | Raster |

**Figure B-4. TGD data model**

## Appendix C

# Terrain Appendix

*This appendix provides guidelines and responsibilities for creating the terrain appendix as part of the engineer annex used in Army plans and orders. Refer to FM 5-0 for more information on planning and orders and FM 3-34 for information on the engineer annex and the engineer unit operation order. See JP 2-03 for information on the GI&S annex (annex M) used in joint orders and plans.*

## GENERAL GUIDELINES

C-1. Plans and orders are critical components to mission command. They foster mission command by clearly conveying the commander's intent, assigning tasks and purposes to subordinates, and providing the minimum coordinating measures necessary to synchronize the operation. To maintain clarity and simplicity, plans and orders include annexes only when necessary and only when they pertain to the entire command. Annexes contain the details of support and synchronization necessary to accomplish the mission.

C-2. Appendixes to mission orders are an information management tool. Appendixes contain information necessary to expand annexes. The engineer annex contains information not included in the base order or other annexes that enables subordinates' planning and successful mission execution. It does not include instructions or orders directly for engineer units, but covers critical aspects of the entire engineer plan.

C-3. Information pertaining to the geospatial engineering mission is provided in appendix 3 (Terrain) to the engineer annex. This information aims at unifying the geospatial effort applied at the various echelons, especially with regard to the generation and flow of geospatial data, and the management of geospatial databases. Appendix 3 serves as the primary source for general information about the military significance of the terrain (OAKOC) and its general effects on the operation. More specific information on the operational impacts of the terrain from each of the staff section's perspective is provided in its respective annex, which is enabled by geospatial engineers describing the physical environment (see chapter 1) and by the integration of geospatial engineering through the integrating processes (see chapter 3).

C-4. The format of an appendix is designed to effectively present information and may vary to suit the unit's needs. The terrain appendix example shown in figure C-1, page C-2, follows the five-paragraph format for appendixes prescribed in FM 5-0. The terrain appendix can include any combination of text and graphics to best communicate information to subordinates. Though the format of the terrain appendix can vary, it should meet the following general criteria:

- Contains all critical information and tasks pertaining to the geospatial engineering effort not covered elsewhere in the order.
- Does not contain items covered in SOPs unless the mission requires a change to the SOP.
- Provides information that is clear and concise.
- Includes only information and instructions that have been fully coordinated in other parts of the plan or order.

## RESPONSIBILITIES

C-5. The ENCOORD and the geospatial engineer share in the responsibilities for integrating GI and products. Following is a detailed description of their responsibilities.

### ENGINEER COORDINATOR

C-6. As the primary staff integrator for the engineer functions, the ENCOORD ensures that the optimal amount of information and the necessary tools are provided in mission plans and orders to facilitate subordinate engineers' planning. The information provided centers on stating the "what" and "why," but not the "how," and serves as the foundational information necessary for subordinates to initiate planning and helps focus their attention without limiting their independent analysis and intuition. The ENCOORD also coordinates with the rest of the staff to ensure that engineer-related information and instructions contained in the base order and the various attachments are consistent. The ENCOORD, the senior geospatial engineer, and the S-2/G-2 work to effectively integrate GI and geospatial products in mission plans and orders.

## SENIOR GEOSPATIAL ENGINEER

C-7. The senior geospatial engineer in each headquarters is responsible for the quality of GI presented in mission orders. The senior geospatial engineer works closely with the ENCOORD and S-2/G-2 in presenting relevant GI in plans and orders in a way to ensure that it is understandable by subordinates and facilitates their mission planning and execution.

C-8. Information and instructions presented to subordinate geospatial engineering teams should alert them to areas requiring more detailed examination. It should also specify the gaps in geospatial data and GI and clearly state responsibilities for fulfilling them.

---

**[Classification]**

(Place the required classification at the top and bottom of every page of the appendix.)

**APPENDIX 3 (TERRAIN) TO ANNEX F (ENGINEER) TO OPERATION ORDER NO_____.**

**References:**

**1. SITUATION.** Include information affecting the geospatial engineering effort that is not covered in the base order or the engineer annex.

  **a. Enemy Forces.** Include a detailed description of enemy GI&S capabilities and how they may be employed to support the enemy mission or objectives. Refer to annex B (Intelligence) as necessary.

  **b. Friendly Forces.** State the higher headquarters concept for geospatial engineering support. List national agencies and higher headquarters capabilities that can provide geospatial products and services.

  **c. Environment.**

    **(1) Terrain.**

- Provide a general description of the characteristics of the terrain (hydrology, surface configuration, soil composition, vegetation, obstacles, and man-made features) in the operational area or specified AO.
- Generally describe the military significance of the terrain (OAKOC).
- This information may be enclosed as a tab to this appendix. Refer to appendix 1 (Intelligence Estimate) to annex B (Intelligence) as necessary.

    **(2) Weather.** Describe how the climate or weather will generally affect the terrain. Refer to appendix 4 (Weather) to annex B as necessary.

    **(3) Civil Considerations.** Describe contractor, nongovernmental organizations, and HN GI&S capabilities that can support operations.

**[Classification]**

---

**Figure C-1. Example of a terrain appendix**

[Classification]

d. **Attachments and Detachments.** List all geospatial engineer assets attached or detached, as necessary, to clarify the task organization.

2. **MISSION.** State the geospatial engineering mission in support of the operation.

3. **EXECUTION.**

a. **Concept of Support.** Describe how geospatial engineering capabilities will support the operation. Supplement the scheme of engineer operations in annex F (Engineer) with any additional information that clarifies the geospatial engineering tasks, purposes, and priorities in support of each phase of the scheme of maneuver. The four primary functions of geospatial engineering (generate, analyze, manage, and disseminate) may be used to structure this narrative.

b. **Tasks to Subordinate Units.** List the geospatial engineer tasks to be accomplished by a specific subordinate unit that are not included in the base order. Provide task and purpose for specific geospatial engineer assets that are task-organized to a subordinate unit, only as necessary to ensure unity of effort.

c. **Coordinating Instructions.** Include—

- Critical geospatial engineer instructions for subordinate geospatial engineer teams or elements for each of the major functions (generate, manage, analyze, disseminate).
- GI requirements (by priority) that must be considered or reported by subordinate geospatial engineer elements.
- RFIs submitted to higher and adjacent units. Refer to annex L (ISR) as required for GI requirements tasked to ISR collection assets.
- Channels for using reachback.
- Technical channels for contacting contractors and other support agencies regarding technical assistance with geospatial automated systems.
- Instructions for disseminating and storing GI and products.
- Instructions for establishing, updating, standardizing, and synchronizing geospatial databases.

4. **SERVICE SUPPORT.** List any unique geospatial engineering service support (for example, augmenting NST or contractor support requirements) not addressed in either the base order or annex F. Describe basic loads of GI&S stocks to be maintained by subordinates. Provide information (stock numbers) and describe the appropriate channels for ordering and distributing geospatial products and supplies for printing and reproduction. Refer to annex I (Service Support) as necessary.

5. **COMMAND AND SIGNAL.** Identify ABCS control hierarchy for the common user network. Provide other pertinent information pertaining to networks and databases needed to support GI&S operations.

ACKNOWLEDGE: (if distributed separately from base order)

[Authenticator's last name]
[Authenticator's grade]

TABS:

DISTRIBUTION: (if distributed separately from the base order)

[Classification]

Legend:
ABCS – Army Battle Command System
AO – area of operations
GI – geospatial information
GI&S – geospatial information and services
HN – host nation

ISR – intelligence, surveillance, and reconnaissance
NST – National Geospatial-Intelligence Agency
OAKOC – observation and fields of fire, avenues of approach, key terrain, obstacles, and cover and concealment
RFI – request for information

**Figure C-1. Example of a terrain appendix (continued)**

This page intentionally left blank.

# Characteristics of Terrain

As discussed in chapter 1, terrain analysis is conducted to study the natural and man-made features in an area and evaluate their effects on military operations. This appendix describes the six characteristics of terrain (hydrology, surface configuration, soil composition, vegetation, obstacles, and man-made features) that geospatial engineers address during terrain analysis. These six characteristics serve as the framework for describing the terrain in an operational area or a specific AO.

## HYDROLOGY

D-1. Water is an essential commodity and is always an important factor in planning. It is necessary for drinking, sanitation, food preparation, construction, and decontamination. Support activities, such as helicopter maintenance and the operation of medical facilities, consume large volumes of water. When untreated or stagnant, water can present health hazards. Drainage features, such as streams and rivers, can affect mobility and shape COAs. Engineers play an important role in providing water to Army forces and are responsible for finding subsurface water; drilling wells; and constructing, repairing, or maintaining water facilities. Geospatial engineers generate, manage, and analyze hydrologic data and work with ground-survey teams and well-drilling teams to locate water sources. Geospatial engineers also produce GI to help commanders and staffs understand the effects of surface drainage (streams and rivers) on operations.

### SOURCES OF WATER

D-2. Water availability and consumption requirements vary based on the climate and topography of a region and the type and scope of operations. Through terrain analysis, geospatial engineers can help planners determine probable sources of water that can exist on and below the surface.

### Surface Water

D-3. Surface water is commonly selected for use in the field because it is the most accessible; however, it tends to be more contaminated than groundwater. Surface water resources are generally more accessible and adequate in plains and plateaus than in mountains. Large amounts of good quality water can normally be obtained in coastal areas, valleys, or alluvial and glacial plains. Although large quantities are available in delta plains, the water may be brackish or salty. Water supplies are scarce on lacustrine, loess, volcanic, and karst plains. Large springs are the best sources of water in karstic plains and plateaus. In the plains of arid regions, water usually cannot be obtained in quantities required by modern armies, and when it is, it is usually highly mineralized. In the plains and plateaus of humid tropical regions, surface water is abundant but is generally polluted and requires treatment. Perennial surface water supplies are difficult to obtain in arctic regions; in summer they are abundant, but often polluted.

### Groundwater

D-4. Groundwater is usually less contaminated than surface water and therefore is typically a more desirable water source. In arid environments, exploring and using groundwater can reduce the need to transport water to desired locations. Groundwater is easily obtained from unconsolidated or poorly consolidated materials in alluvial valleys and plains, streams and coastal terraces, glacial outwash plains, and alluvial basins in mountainous regions. Areas of sedimentary and permeable igneous rocks may have fair-to-excellent aquifers, although they usually do not provide as much groundwater as areas composed of unconsolidated materials. Large amounts of good-quality groundwater may be obtained at shallow depths from the alluvial plains of valleys and coasts and in somewhat greater depths in their terraces. Aquifers underlying the surface of inland sedimentary plains and basins also provide adequate amounts of water. Abundant quantities of good-quality water generally can be obtained from shallow to deep wells in glacial plains. In loess plains and plateaus, small amounts of water may be secured from shallow wells, but these supplies are apt to fluctuate seasonally. Plains and plateaus in arid climates generally yield small, highly mineralized quantities of groundwater. In semiarid climates, following a severe drought, dry streambeds frequently can yield considerable amounts of excellent subsurface water. Groundwater is abundant in the plains of humid tropical regions, but it is typically polluted. In arctic and subarctic plains, wells and springs fed by groundwater above the permafrost are dependable only in summer; some of the sources freeze in winter, and subterranean channels and outlets may shift in location.

D-5. Wells may yield large quantities of water if they tap into underground streams. Wells that penetrate aquifers within or below the permafrost are good sources of perennial supply. Adequate supplies of groundwater are hard to obtain in hills and mountains composed of gneiss, granite, and granitelike rocks. They may contain springs and shallow wells that generally yield water in small amounts. Shallow wells in low-lying lava plains normally produce large quantities of groundwater. In lava uplands, water is more difficult to find, wells are harder to develop, and careful prospecting is necessary to obtain adequate supplies. In wells near the seacoast, excessive withdrawal of freshwater may lower the water table, allowing infiltration of saltwater that ruins the well and the surrounding aquifer. Springs and wells near the base of volcanic cones may yield fair quantities of water, but elsewhere in volcanic cones the groundwater is too far below the surface for drilling to be practicable. See FM 5-484 for more information on the ability of rocks and soils to hold and transmit water.

D-6. Vegetation is a good indicator of groundwater sources. Deciduous trees tend to have far-reaching root systems indicating a water table close to the ground surface, while coniferous trees tend to have deep root systems indicating the water table is farther away from the ground surface. Palm trees indicate water within 2 or 3 feet, salt grass indicates water within 6 feet, and cottonwood and willow trees indicate water within 10 to 12 feet. The common sage, greasewood, and cactus do not indicate water levels. Other indicators of potential groundwater include—

- Crop irrigation.
- Karst topography.
- Snowmelt patterns.
- Wetlands.
- Springs.
- Soil moisture.
- Surface water.
- Wells and qanats.
- Urban areas.

## SURFACE DRAINAGE

D-7. Surface drainage can significantly impact military operations. It can impede CCM, restrict movements to roads, and render land areas that are prone to flooding unsuitable for positioning forces or capabilities. Planners must first analyze the flow and channeling characteristic of surface water that varies based on geographic location and seasonal weather patterns. Drainage features can be perennial (containing water most of the year), intermittent (containing water part of the year), or dry or cyclical (usually dry, such as wadis). Planners can then determine the effects of surface water on operations based on the capabilities of personnel, vehicles, and equipment. Geospatial engineers enable this analysis by acquiring or generating surface drainage data that include such things as width and depth of streams and canals and the velocity and discharge of streams. They also obtain or produce information on dams, levees, and other drainage features and can create geospatial products that show the catastrophic effects if they fail.

D-8. In the absence of geologic maps and data, drainage patterns can be studied to determine rock types and better understand an area's structure and composition. The most common drainage patterns are shown in figure D-1.

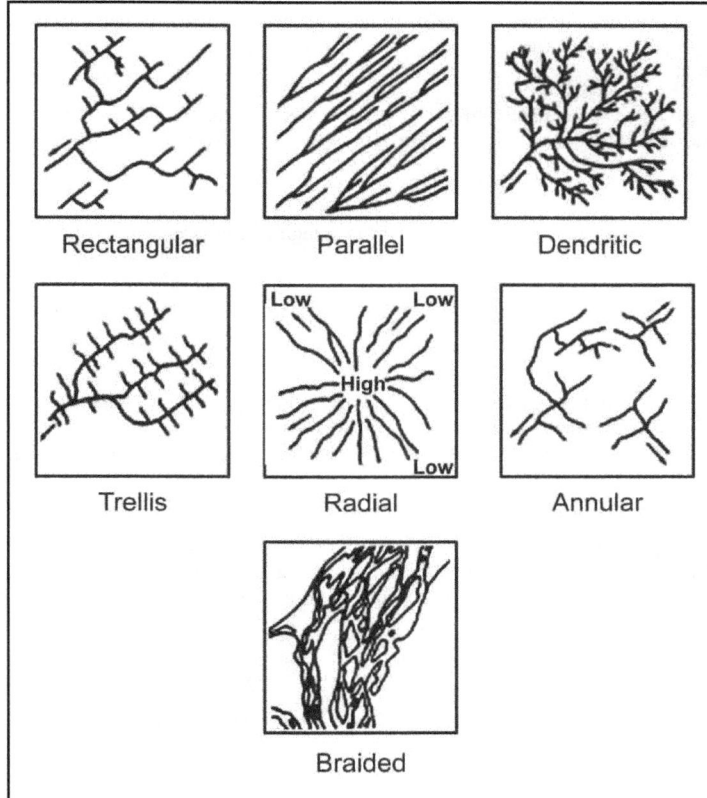

**Figure D-1. Common drainage patterns**

**Rectangular**

D-9. The rectangular drainage pattern, characterized by abrupt bends in streams, develops where a treelike drainage pattern prevails over a broad region and is generally associated with massive igneous rock. Metamorphic rock surfaces, particularly those composed of schist and slate, commonly have rectangular drainage. Slate possesses a particularly finely textured system. Its drainage pattern is extremely angular and has easily recognizable short gullies that are locally parallel.

**Parallel**

D-10. In the parallel pattern, major streams flow side by side in the direction of the regional slope. Parallel streams are indicative of gently dipping beds or uniformly sloping topography. The greater the slope, the more nearly parallel the drainage and the straighter the flow. Local areas of lava flows often have parallel drainage, even though the regional pattern may be radial. Alluvial fans may also exhibit parallel drainage, but the pattern may be locally influenced by faults or jointing. Coastal plains, because of their slope toward the sea, develop parallel drainage overboard regions.

**Dendritic**

D-11. The dendritic drainage pattern is a treelike pattern composed of branching tributaries to a main stream, characteristic of essentially flat-lying and homogeneous rocks. This pattern implies that the area was originally flat and is composed of relatively uniform materials. Dendritic drainage is also typical of glacial till, tidal marshes, and localized areas in sandy coastal plains. The difference in texture or density of a dendritic pattern may help identify surface materials and organic areas.

### Trellis

D-12. In a trellis pattern, the mainstream runs parallel, and small streams flow and join at right angles. This pattern is found in areas where sedimentary or metamorphic rocks have been folded.

### Radial

D-13. In a radial pattern, streams flow outward from a high central area. This pattern is found on domes, volcanic cones, and round hills. However, the sides of a dome or volcano might have a radial drainage system while the pattern inside a volcanic cone might be centripetal, converging toward the center of the depression.

### Annular

D-14. The annular pattern is a modified form of the radial drainage system, found where sedimentary rocks are upturned by a dome structure. In this pattern, streams circle around a high central area. The granitic dome drainage channels may follow a circular path around the base of the dome when it is surrounded by tilted beds.

### Braided

D-15. A braided stream pattern commonly forms in arid areas during flash flooding. The stream attempts to carry more material than it is capable of handling. Much of the gravel and sand is deposited as bars and islands in the stream bed.

## SURFACE CONFIGURATION

D-16. Surface configuration is the physical shape of the terrain and includes—
- Elevation.
- Depressions.
- Slope.
- Landform type.
- Surface roughness.

D-17. Elevation of a point on the earth's surface is the vertical distance it is above or below mean sea level. Relief is the representation of the shapes of hills, valleys, streams, or terrain features on the earth's surface. Local relief is the difference in elevation between points in a given area. The elevations or irregularities of a land surface are represented on graphics by contours, hypsometric tints, shading, spot elevations, and hachures.

D-18. The rate of rise or fall of a terrain feature is known as its slope. Slope affects the speed at which equipment or personnel can move. Slope can be categorized as gentle, steep, concave, or convex (FM 3-25.26) and can be expressed as the slope ratio or gradient, the angle of slope, or the percent of slope. The slope ratio is a fraction in which the vertical distance (rise) is the numerator and the horizontal distance (run) is the denominator. The angle of slope in degrees is the angular difference the inclined surface makes with the horizontal plane. The tangent of the slope angle is determined by dividing the vertical distance by the horizontal distance between the highest and lowest elevations of the inclined surface. The actual angle is found by using trigonometric tables. The percent of slope is the number of meters of elevation per 100 meters of horizontal distance. Slope information that is available to the analyst in degrees or in ratio values may be converted to percent of slope by using a nomogram.

D-19. Landforms are the physical expression of the land surface and are generally categorized into the following groups:
- Plains.

- Plateaus.
- Hills.
- Mountains.

D-20. Within each of these groups are surface features of a smaller size, such as flat lowlands and valleys. Each type results from the interaction of earth processes in a region with given climate and rock conditions. A complete study of landform includes determination of its size, shape, arrangement, surface configuration, and relationship to the surrounding area.

# SOIL COMPOSITION

D-21. Planners rely heavily on the results of soil analysis, since variations in soil composition (soil type, drainage characteristics, and moisture content) can affect trafficability, road and airfield construction, and the ease of digging fighting positions in a specific area. Generating soil data normally requires extensive field sampling and the expertise of soil analysts. Once the data are acquired, geospatial engineers use these in combination with standard geospatial products and imagery to create tailored geospatial products (such as the soil trafficability overlay shown in figure A-12, page A-13) that enables the staff to further its own analysis of the operational area or specific AO and facilitate planning. The effectiveness of these products is directly related to the quality of available soil data. See FM 5-410 for more information.

D-22. For field identification and classification, soil is grouped into the following five major categories:

- Gravel.
- Sand.
- Silt.
- Clay.
- Organic matter.

D-23. These soil types seldom exist separately. They are usually found in mixtures of various proportions which contribute to its unique characteristics. Some soils may gain strength under traffic (compaction), while others lose it.

## GRAVEL

D-24. Gravel is angular to rounded, bulky rock particles ranging in size from about 0.6 to 7.6 centimeters (¼ to 3 inches) in diameter. It is classified as coarse or fine; well or poorly graded; and angular, flat, or rounded. Next to solid bedrock, well-graded and compacted gravel is the most stable natural foundation material. Weather has little or no effect on its trafficability. It offers excellent traction for tracked vehicles; however, if not mixed with other soil, the loose particles may roll under pressure, hampering the movement of wheeled vehicles.

## SAND

D-25. Sand consists of angular or rounded rock grains that are 0.6 centimeter (¼ inch) in diameter and smaller and is classified as coarse, medium, or fine. Well-graded angular sand is desirable for concrete aggregate and for foundation material. It is easy to drain and ordinarily not affected by frost action or moisture. Analysts must be careful in distinguishing fine sand from silt. When sand is wet enough to become compacted or when mixed with clay, it provides excellent trafficability. Very dry, loose sand is an obstacle to vehicles, especially on slopes. Under wet conditions, remoldable sands react to traffic as do fine-grained soils.

## SILT

D-26. Silt is soil- or rock-derived granular material of a grain size between sand and clay. It lacks plasticity and possesses little or no cohesion when dry. Because of silt's instability, water will cause it to become soft or to change to a "quick" condition. When dry, silt provides excellent trafficability, although it is very dusty. However, it absorbs water quickly and turns to a deep, soft mud (a quick condition), which impedes movement. When groundwater or seepage is present, silt exposed to frost action is subject to ice accumulation and consequent heaving.

## CLAY

D-27. Clay generally consists of microscopic particles. Its plasticity and adhesiveness are excellent characteristics. Depending on mineral composition and proportion of coarser grains, clays vary from lean (low plasticity) to fat (high plasticity). Many clays which are brittle or stiff in their undisturbed state become soft and plastic when worked. When thoroughly dry, clay provides a hard surface with excellent trafficability; however, it is seldom dry except in arid climates. It absorbs water very slowly but takes a long time to dry and is very sticky and slippery. Slopes with a clay surface are difficult or impassable, and deep ruts form rapidly on level ground. A combination of silt and clay makes a particularly poor surface when wet.

## ORGANIC MATTER

D-28. Chemically deposited and organic sediments are classified on the basis of mode and source of sedimentations. The identification of highly organic soil is relatively easy. It contains partially decayed grass, twigs, and leaves and has a characteristic dark brown to black color, a spongy feel, and fibrous texture.

D-29. Geospatial engineers use the two-letter abbreviations established in the Unified Soil Classification System to describe soil. The primary letters identify the predominant soil fraction, which are—

- **G** – gravel.
- **S** – sand.
- **C** – clay (used only with fine-grained soil with 50 percent fines or greater).
- **M** – silt.
- **O** – organic.

D-30. The secondary letters further describe the characteristics of the predominant soil fraction. The percent of gravel, sand, and frees provides the information necessary to choose the primary letter. The secondary letters are—

- **W** – well-graded (used to describe sands containing less than 12 percent fines).
- **P** – poorly graded.
- **M** – silty fines (used with sands and gravels containing less than 5 percent but more than or equal to 50 percent frees).
- **C** – clay-based fines.
- **L** – low compressibility (used to describe fine-grained soils [silts, clays, organics]).
- **H** – high compressibility.

# VEGETATION

D-31. Geospatial engineers generate and analyze vegetation data and create geospatial products to show the effects of vegetation on vehicular and foot movements, landing zones, drop zones, observation, and cover and concealment.

D-32. The types of vegetation in an area can give an indication of the climatic conditions, soil, drainage, and water supply. Geospatial engineers focus their terrain analysis on these types of vegetation—trees, scrubs and shrubs, grasses, and crops.

D-33. Trees can provide good cover and concealment and can also impede movement and maneuver. Large trees are usually spaced far enough apart to allow the passage of vehicles, but this gap is often filled with smaller trees or brush that must be considered. Small trees are usually spaced closer together and do not offer a gap for vehicles; however, depending on their diameter, they can be pushed over by large tracked vehicles. Trees that have been pushed over tend to pile up and can block follow-on vehicles. Trees that are large enough to stop wheeled vehicles are usually too closely spaced to allow passage.

D-34. Trees are classified as either deciduous (broadleaf) or coniferous (evergreen). With the exception of species growing in tropical areas and a few species existing in temperate climates, most broadleaf trees lose their leaves in the fall and become dormant until early spring. Needle leaf trees do not normally lose their leaves and exhibit only small seasonal changes. Woodlands or forests are classified according to the dominant type of tree in them. A forest is classified as either deciduous or coniferous if it contains at least 60 percent of that species. Wooded areas that contain less than a 60 percent mixture of either species are classified as a mixed forest. Scrubs include a variety of trees that have had their growth stunted because of soil or climatic conditions. Shrubs comprise the undergrowth in open forests, but in arid and semiarid areas they are the dominant vegetation. Shrubs are normally not considered an obstacle to movement and provide good concealment from ground observation; however, they may restrict fields of fire. As part of terrain analysis, grass more than 1 meter high is considered tall and may provide concealment for dismounted troops. Grass can improve the trafficability of soils.

D-35. Field crops represent the predominant class of cultivated vegetation. The size of cultivated areas ranges from paddies covering a quarter of an acre to vast wheat fields extending for thousands of acres. In a concentrated agricultural area where all arable land is used for the crop producing the highest yield, predictions on the nature of the soil in that area can be made based on information about the predominant crop. For example, rice requires fine-textured soils, while other crops generally must have firm, well-drained land. An area containing orchards or plantations usually consists of rows of evenly spaced trees, showing evidence of planned planting, which can be distinguished in aerial imagery. These areas are usually free of underbrush and vines. Rice fields are flooded areas surrounded by low dikes or walls. Some crops, such as grain, improve the trafficability of soils, while others, such as vineyards, present a tangled maze of poles and wires and create obstacles to vehicles and dismounted troops. Wheeled vehicles and some tracked vehicles are unable to cross flooded paddy fields, although they may be negotiated when the fields are drained and dry or frozen. Sown crops, such as wheat, barley, oats, and rye, are grown on a flat surface and have a different impact on movement and concealment than crops planted in furrows.

# OBSTACLES

D-36. Obstacles are any physical characteristics of the terrain that impede the mobility of a force. All obstacles are either existing or reinforcing. Existing obstacles are inherent aspects of the terrain and can be natural, man-made, or a combination of both. Examples of natural obstacles include rivers, forests, and steep slopes. Examples of man-made obstacles include buildings and structures. Reinforcing obstacles are obstacles specifically constructed, emplaced, or detonated by military forces and are categorized as tactical or protective. See FM 90-7 for more information on reinforcing obstacles.

D-37. Obstacles can have varying degrees of impact on different types of movement, such as ground (mounted or dismounted) or air or on different types of vehicles, such as wheeled or tracked. Obstacles to air mobility include mountains; power lines; or tall buildings that exceed an aircraft's service ceiling, restrict nap-of-the-earth flight, or that force an aircraft to employ a particular flight profile. The obstacle analysis performed by geospatial engineers provides the foundation for the staff's further analysis of the effects of obstacles and the assessment of the operational impacts based on their areas of expertise. As discussed in chapter 1, geospatial engineers describe the terrain to the staff using geospatial products (such as the COO) that facilitate the staff's further analysis of the OE.

# MAN-MADE FEATURES

D-38. Man-made features generally exist in, near, and between urban areas. The level of detail in describing man-made features will depend on the mission and the level of planning. In support of urban operations at the lower tactical levels, geospatial engineers must provide a greater degree of emphasis on the 3-D nature of the topography (supersurface, surface, and subsurface areas). Advancements in automated geospatial applications, such as the UTP developed by the AGC, provide more detailed GI and better visualization of the urban environment. An example of a UTP product is shown in appendix A (figure A-22, page A-23). See FM 3-06 for more information on analyzing an urban environment.

D-39. Man-made features can be grouped into broad, functional categories to help organize the results of analysis and describe the terrain. These functional areas include—

- Industrial.
- Transportation.
- Commercial and recreational.
- Residential.
- Communication.
- Governmental and institutional.
- Military.

## INDUSTRIAL

D-40. Industrial areas and facilities are used in the extraction, processing, and production of intermediate and finished products or raw materials. Examples include factories, warehouses, power plants, and oil refineries. Manufacturing plants are categorized as either heavy or medium/light. Heavy-manufacturing plants contain distinctive structures, such as blast furnaces, while medium and light plants are usually housed in general loft buildings from which machinery can be removed. Industrial areas often develop on the outskirts of urban areas where commercial transportation is easiest. These areas may provide ideal sites for sustainment bases and maintenance sites.

## TRANSPORTATION

D-41. Transportation areas and facilities are used in moving materials and people. Geospatial engineers evaluate transportation features (networks and facilities) to determine their effects on likely operations. This includes, but is not limited to, all highways, railways, and waterways over which troops or supplies can be moved.

### Roads

D-42. FM 3-34.170 provides information on road classification and describes important road characteristics and limiting factors considered during route reconnaissance. Road characteristics (see figure D-2) include—

- Minimum traveled-way width.
- Road surface material.
- Obstructions.
  - Bridges and culverts.
  - Overpasses.
  - Cuts and fills.
- Restrictions.
  - Grades.
  - Curves.
  - Load-bearing.

D-43. Roads are categorized within the following (see table D-1):

- All-weather, dual/divided highway.
- All-weather, hard-surface.
- All-weather, loose-surface.
- Fair-weather, loose-surface.
- Car track.

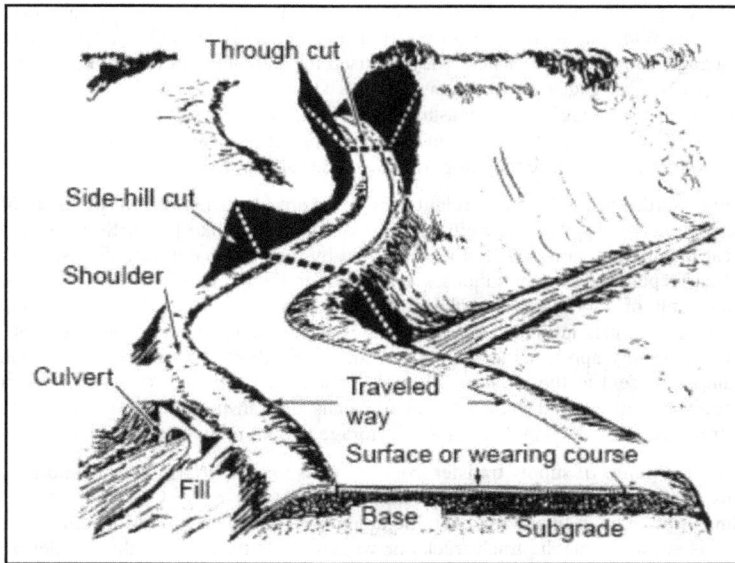

**Figure D-2. Road components**

**Table D-1. Description of road categories**

| Road Categories | Description |
|---|---|
| All-weather, dual/divided highway | • Waterproof surface paved with concrete, bituminous surfacing, brick, or paving stone.<br>• Slightly affected by precipitation and temperature changes. |
| All-weather, hard-surface | • Waterproof surface paved with concrete, bituminous surfacing, brick, or paving stone.<br>• Slightly affected by precipitation and temperature changes. |
| All-weather, loose-surface | • Constructed of crushed rock, gravel, or smoothed earth with an oil coating.<br>• Graded and drained, but not waterproof.<br>• Can be considerably affected by rain, frost, or thaw.<br>• May collapse completely under heavy use during adverse weather conditions. |
| Fair-weather, loose-surface | • Constructed of natural or stabilized soil, sand clay, shell, cinders, or disintegrated granite or rock.<br>• Includes logging road, abandoned roads, and corduroy roads.<br>• Can become quickly impassable in adverse weather. |
| Cart track | • Natural traveled ways including caravan routes and winter roads.<br>• Too narrow to accommodate four-wheeled military vehicles. |

**Railways**

D-44. Railways can be a highly desirable adjunct to extended military operations. Railroads include all fixed property belonging to a line, such as land, permanent way, and facilities necessary for the movement of traffic and protection of the permanent way. They include bridges, tunnels, and other structures. Railway analysis covers all physical characteristics and critical features of the existing system and includes components such as roadbed, ballast, track, rails, and horizontal and vertical alignment.

D-45. The gage of a railroad is the distance between the rails. Railroad gages are classified as wide, standard, or narrow. Wide gages are 5 feet or wider. They are mostly used by Russian, Finnish, and Spanish lines. Standard gages are 4 feet 8½ inches. They are used for main and branch lines in the United States and the rest of Europe. Narrow gages are less than standard. Their use is somewhat limited to and usually found in mountainous, industrial, logging, and coastal defense areas and in mines and supply dumps. In South and Central America, the one-meter gage is found in many places; however, many of the countries are now adopting the standard gage because they import U.S.-made rolling stock.

D-46. Marshaling yards are used to sort freight cars. They are identified by a large group of parallel tracks with a restricted (one- or two-track) entrance and exit called a choke point. Service yards are normally found in or near marshaling yards and can be identified by the presence of roundhouses, turntables, service facilities, and car repair shops. Roundhouses are used for light repair and storage of locomotives. The number of roof vents on top of the roundhouse indicates the capacity of the roundhouse. Turntables are used for turning the engines around. Service facilities include coal towers, water towers, and coal piles. Car-repair shops normally appear as long, low buildings straddling one or more tracks, with cars awaiting repairs on sidings adjacent to the buildings. Freight or loading yards are identified by loading platforms, freight stations, warehouses, and access to other means of transportation. Special loading stations are identified by grain elevators, coal and ore bins, oil storage tanks, and livestock pens with loading ramps.

D-47. Railheads are points of supply transfer from railroads to other transportation and are generally found in small towns or cities where sidings and storage space already exist. Characteristics of a railhead are spurs and sidings from a main line; a road net, including narrow gage railroads, leading away from the area; piles of materials stacked near the track trucks or wagons or both, either without order or organized into convoys or trains; and temporary dwellings, such as tents or Quonset™ huts, for housing troops guarding and handling supplies.

## Bridges and Culverts

D-48. All bridges present a potential restriction to traffic. Important feature data include—

- Location.
- Type of gap being crossed.
- Overall length.
- Roadway width.
- Horizontal and vertical clearance.
- Military load classification (MLC).
- Number and length of spans.
- Type of span construction.
- Bypasses.

D-49. The common types of bridges are shown in figure D-3. See FM 3-34.170 for information on specific bridge characteristics used in determining bridge classification.

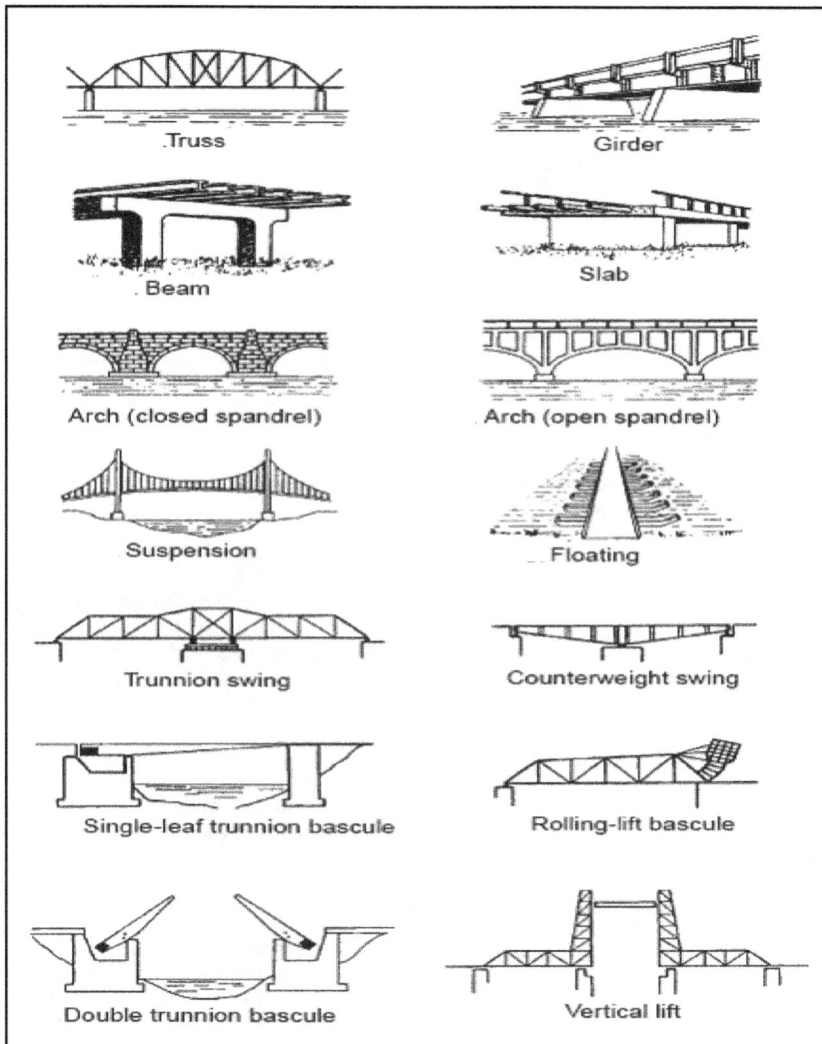

**Figure D-3. Common types of bridges**

D-50. Culverts are grouped into the following four main categories:
- Pipe (most common).
- Box.
- Arch.
- Rail girder spans.

D-51. Culverts are usually concrete, but corrugated metal and cast iron are also used. The pipes have different shapes and can range from 12 inches to several feet in diameter. Box culverts are used to a great extent in modern construction. They are rectangular in cross section and usually concrete. A large box culvert is similar to a slab bridge. Arch culverts were used frequently in the past but are rarely constructed now. They are concrete, masonry, brick, or timber. Rail girder spans are found on lightly built railways or, in an emergency, on any line. The rails are laid side by side and keyed head to base and may be used for spans of 3 meters or less.

## Tunnels

D-52. A tunnel is an artificially covered (such as a covered bridge) or an underground section of road along a route. Important characteristics of tunnels include location, type, length, horizontal clearance, overhead clearance, alignment, and gradient. See FM 3-34.170 for more information on tunnel types and characteristics.

## Ferries

D-53. Ferries convey traffic and cargo across a water feature. These vessels vary widely in physical appearance and capacity depending on the depth, width, and current of the stream and on the characteristics of traffic to be moved. The capacity of a ferry boat is usually expressed in tons and total number of passengers and is sometimes assigned an MLC number. Climatic conditions have a marked effect on ferry conditions. Tide fluctuations, fog, ice, floods, and excessive dry spells can reduce the total traffic-moving capacity and increase the hazard of the water route. A ferry site is the place where ferries convey traffic and cargo. Important information about ferry sites includes the width and depth of the water barrier and the conditions of the approaches (such as clearance and load-bearing). FM 3-34.170 contains information on ferry reconnaissance and reporting.

## Fords

D-54. A *ford* is a shallow part of a body of water or wet gap that can be crossed without bridging, boats, ferries, or rafts. It is a location in a water barrier where the physical characteristics of current, bottom, and approaches permit the passage of personnel, vehicles, and other equipment where the wheels or tracks remain in contact with the bottom at all times (FM 3-90.12). Fords are classified according to their crossing potential, or trafficability, for foot or wheeled and tracked vehicles. The ford's stream-bottom composition largely determines its trafficability. In some cases, the natural river bottom of a ford may have been improved to increase load-bearing capacity and to reduce the water depth. Improved fords may have gravel or concrete surfacing, layers of sandbags, metal screening or matting, or timber or wooden planking. The composition and slope of approaches to a ford also affect trafficability. Approaches may be paved with concrete or bituminous surface material, but they are usually unimproved and can be affected by inclement weather and vehicle traffic. Climatic conditions (such as seasonal floods and excessive dry seasons) and the velocity of the current and the presence of debris are also important factors in assessing stream fordability. FM 3-34.170 contains information on ford reconnaissance and reporting.

D-55. Low-water bridges consist of two or more intermediate supports with concrete decking and are located entirely in ravines or gullies. During high-water periods, they are easily confused with paved fords because both are completely submerged. It is important to know the difference between this type of bridge and a paved ford because of corresponding military load limitations.

## Pipelines

D-56. Pipelines that carry petroleum and natural gas are an important mode of transportation. White rail, water, and road transport are used extensively for transporting fluids and gases. The overland movement of petroleum and refined products is performed most economically and expeditiously by pipeline. Crude-oil pipelines are used only to transport crude oil, while many refined-product pipelines carry more than one product. These products are sent through the pipelines in tenders, or batches, to keep the amount of mixing to a minimum. Because of their most vital link in an industrialized country's energy supply system, coal and ore are also carried in pipelines as slurry.

D-57. Pipelines can exist above or below ground and may extend cross-country or follow the alignment of roads and railroads. When a pipeline crosses a stream or river, it is usually run along the stream bottom. Where streams are swift or where beds may shift rapidly, the pipe can be attached to existing bridges or special pipeline suspension bridges. Siphon crossings are used where necessary. When an increase or decrease of pressure is required, regulating features such as pumps or compressors are used. Pumping stations are used for liquid fuels and compressor stations for gas. They are similar in appearance except for the cooling towers present at compressor stations.

D-58. Valves, manifolds, and meters are integral parts of any pipeline system and are located at frequent intervals along the pipeline and at terminals. Valves protruding from the ground are often the only indicators of a pipeline alignment.

## Ports and Harbors

D-59. Ports are areas along seacoasts, navigable rivers, or inland waterways where ships may discharge or receive their cargoes. Principal port facilities are berthing space, storage space, cargo-handling equipment, cargo transshipment facilities, and vessel-servicing facilities. Ports may have various structures affording berthing space or may be any place a vessel may be made fast. These structures include piers, moles, and wharves or quays. Piers project into the water at an angle with the shoreline. Piers are supported by pilings driven into the harbor bottom, while moles are of solid construction. Wharves and quays are parallel with the shoreline, while piers and moles are perpendicular to it. The majority of landing structures are either piers or wharves.

D-60. Harbors are areas where the anchorage and shore are protected from the sea and storms by natural or man-made barriers (such as seawalls, breakwaters, jetties, and moles). Areas that do not have this protection but are still suitable for vessel anchorage are open anchorages or roadsteads. A good harbor consists of deep water, adequate protection from storms, enough space to accommodate large numbers of vessels, and a shoreline that can be developed as a port and as a site for industry. Harbors may be situated on the sea, estuaries, or inland lakes and rivers.

D-61. Important factors concerning ports and harbors include water depth, bottom characteristics, tidal fluctuations, discharge volumes and river flow velocity, tidal and river currents, landmark locations, and location of underwater obstacles. Engineers, divers, and other specialists perform surveys to establish basic facts of shoreline, water depth, bottom character, and existing structures (such as harbors and wharves). See FM 5-480 for more information.

D-62. Dredging operations require detailed topographic and hydrographic surveys and data on tidal range, tidal prism, flood stages, velocity, and other hydrographic characteristics, including the status of siltation and scour. Other information requirements include data on bridges, breakwaters, jetties, piers, island, overhead and submarine cables, and type and size of vessels scheduled to use the waterway. See FM 55-50 for more information.

## Airfields and Heliports

D-63. Airfields and heliports are classified by their degree of permanence and type of aircraft (fixed- or rotary-wing) they are designed to support. An airfield consists of runways, taxiways, and parking areas that may be permanent, temporary, or natural. A heliport is an area specifically designated and marked for helicopter landings and takeoffs. The surface of the pad may be natural, temporary, or permanent.

D-64. Runways are the most significant feature of an airfield, and detailed information concerning them, taxiways, and parking areas is essential in properly evaluating an airfield's capabilities. The length, width, load-bearing capabilities, and pavement condition directly influence the type and amount of traffic an airfield can accommodate. Taxiways are access paths to parking aprons, hangar aprons, and handstands or revetments. A parallel taxiway parallels the runway but is usually narrower. Under emergency conditions, it may be used as a runway, but it should not be reported as a runway. Airfield capacity is described by stating the maximum (aircraft) on the ground, which is the maximum number of aircraft (usually expressed in terms of C-141 aircraft) that can be accommodated on an airfield.

D-65. Geospatial engineers, intelligence analysts, and other specialists provide baseline information on available airfields and heliports in the operational area or specific AO based on a broad view early in the planning phase. As required, more specific information is generated from airfield assessments performed by assessment teams, survey teams, or as a result of reconnaissance operations.

## COMMERCIAL AND RECREATIONAL

D-66. Commercial and recreational areas and buildings (such as shopping centers, parking lots, stadiums, and sports fields) are where the major business and recreational activities occur in an urban area. Larger open areas such as parking lots and sport fields can serve as landing zones and artillery firing positions. Large covered areas or areas with some type of containment, such as stadiums and arenas, can provide locations for displaced civilians, interrogation centers, and prisoner-of-war holding facilities.

## RESIDENTIAL

D-67. Residential areas and associated buildings are where civilians live and can be found dispersed throughout an urban area. Large suburban areas (or sprawl) normally form on the outskirts. Residential areas often consist of row houses or single-family dwellings set in a grid or ringed pattern in a planned development project. Schools are often located throughout residential areas.

## COMMUNICATION

D-68. Communication buildings and structures (such as communication towers) are used to transmit information and data from place to place. They provide the means for operating telephone, radio, television, and computer systems.

## GOVERNMENTAL AND INSTITUTIONAL

D-69. Governmental and institutional areas and facilities constitute the seat of legal, administrative, and other governmental functions or serve as public service institutions (such as universities and hospitals) for a country or political subdivision. This wide-ranging category includes embassies, universities, hospitals, police and fire stations, courthouses, and prisons.

## MILITARY

D-70. Military areas and facilities are used for controlling, billeting, training, or transporting military forces. Fortifications and military installations may be found in or near urban areas throughout the world.

# Appendix E

# Geospatial Engineering Organizations

This appendix further describes the geospatial engineering organizations that support each echelon down to BCT as discussed in chapter 2. For information on other engineer organizations see FM 3-34.

## GEOSPATIAL PLANNING CELL

E-1. The GPC consists of a control section, a data management and generation section, and an analysis section as shown in figure E-1, page E-2. The control section provides C2 for the GPC and is structured with a deployable element that can be stationed forward for limited periods of time to support the initial onset of operations. As the theater matures, it reverts to base operations. The data management and generation section has a DTSS–base (DTSS–B) and two DTSS–deployable (DTSS–D) and is primarily responsible for the maintenance of the TGD. The analysis section is equipped with two DTSS–light (DTSS–L), which will transition to DCGS mobile and is responsible for providing terrain analysis support. The GPC ensures that all geospatial data production and extraction standards are met to facilitate NGA acceptance of Army TGD data and enable geospatial data dissemination throughout the geospatial community. Geospatial database management is discussed further in appendix B.

## TOPOGRAPHIC ENGINEER COMPANY

E-2. Topographic engineer companies (see figure E-2, page E-3) include a headquarters platoon, a field maintenance team, and four analysis platoons. As shown in figure E-3, page E-4, each analysis platoon consists of two analysis teams, two data management teams, and one print team. Each analysis team is equipped with a DTSS–L, which will transition to a DCGS mobile and is capable of providing additional terrain analysis support to deployed units or augmenting geospatial engineer teams at each echelon down to BCT. The data management teams are equipped with two DTSS–Ds, which will be replaced with two containerized DCGS deployable server suites and can generate geospatial data from a variety of sources, to include deriving high-resolution elevation and feature data from existing and emerging sensors. The print team provides hard-copy geospatial products to supported units. See appendix F for additional information on DTSS.

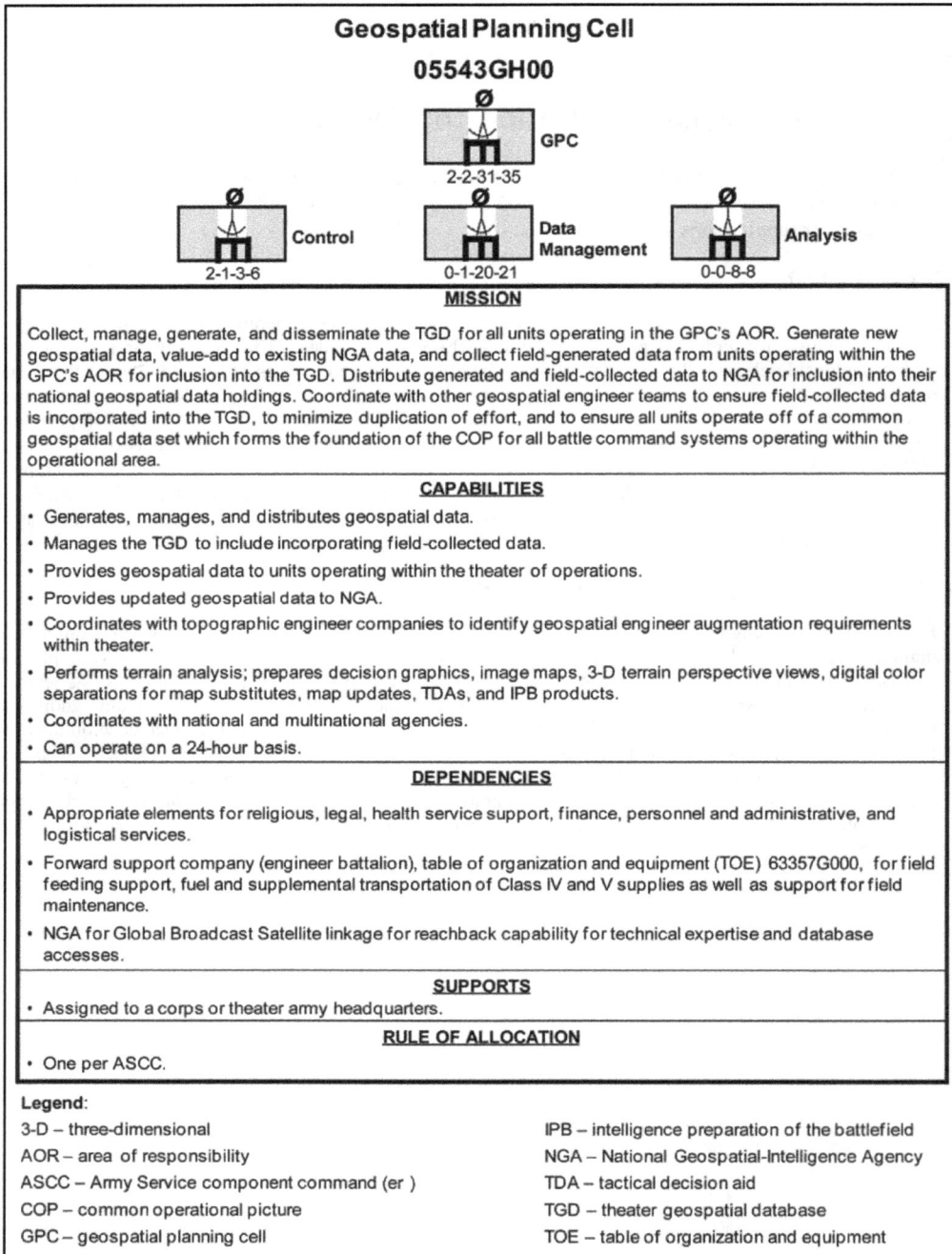

Figure E-1. Geospatial planning cell

---

**Geospatial Planning Cell**

**05543GH00**

GPC
2-2-31-35

Control
2-1-3-6

Data Management
0-1-20-21

Analysis
0-0-8-8

**MISSION**

Collect, manage, generate, and disseminate the TGD for all units operating in the GPC's AOR. Generate new geospatial data, value-add to existing NGA data, and collect field-generated data from units operating within the GPC's AOR for inclusion into the TGD. Distribute generated and field-collected data to NGA for inclusion into their national geospatial data holdings. Coordinate with other geospatial engineer teams to ensure field-collected data is incorporated into the TGD, to minimize duplication of effort, and to ensure all units operate off of a common geospatial data set which forms the foundation of the COP for all battle command systems operating within the operational area.

**CAPABILITIES**

- Generates, manages, and distributes geospatial data.
- Manages the TGD to include incorporating field-collected data.
- Provides geospatial data to units operating within the theater of operations.
- Provides updated geospatial data to NGA.
- Coordinates with topographic engineer companies to identify geospatial engineer augmentation requirements within theater.
- Performs terrain analysis; prepares decision graphics, image maps, 3-D terrain perspective views, digital color separations for map substitutes, map updates, TDAs, and IPB products.
- Coordinates with national and multinational agencies.
- Can operate on a 24-hour basis.

**DEPENDENCIES**

- Appropriate elements for religious, legal, health service support, finance, personnel and administrative, and logistical services.
- Forward support company (engineer battalion), table of organization and equipment (TOE) 63357G000, for field feeding support, fuel and supplemental transportation of Class IV and V supplies as well as support for field maintenance.
- NGA for Global Broadcast Satellite linkage for reachback capability for technical expertise and database accesses.

**SUPPORTS**

- Assigned to a corps or theater army headquarters.

**RULE OF ALLOCATION**

- One per ASCC.

Legend:
3-D – three-dimensional
AOR – area of responsibility
ASCC – Army Service component command (er )
COP – common operational picture
GPC – geospatial planning cell

IPB – intelligence preparation of the battlefield
NGA – National Geospatial-Intelligence Agency
TDA – tactical decision aid
TGD – theater geospatial database
TOE – table of organization and equipment

**Figure E-1. Geospatial planning cell**

## Topographic Engineer Company

### 05610G000

6-4-113-123

Headquarters
2-0-13-15

Analysis
1-1-22-24
(x4)

Field Maintenance Team
0-0-12-12

Headquarters
1-1-2-4

Data Management
0-0-4-4 (x2)

Analysis
0-0-4-4 (x2)

Print
0-0-4-4

### MISSION

Plans, conducts, prepares, and provides management, analysis, and distribution of geospatial data and mobility assessments. Provides division, corps or JTF, theater army, and Federal Emergency Management Agency regions with analysis, collection, generation, management, finishing, and printing capability. Enables protection or consequence management in support of homeland security operations.

### CAPABILITIES

This organization provides the following when all of its subordinate units are organized at Level 1 as shown in their respective TOEs:

- Command and control for the topographic platoons in support of geospatial engineering missions.
- Decision graphics, image maps, 3-D terrain perspective views, map updates, TDAs, and IPB products.
- Personnel and equipment for surge hard-copy production requirements.
- Personnel and equipment for unit-level maintenance of presses.
- Personnel and equipment to Army, corps, division, or other headquarters, as directed, in support of terrain analysis-producing missions.

### DEPENDENCIES

- Appropriate elements for food service; transportation; health service support; religious, legal, finance, personnel, and administrative services; and maintenance of equipment such as light and heavy wheeled vehicles.
- NGA or other NSG topographic data.
- Reachback capability to technical expertise.

### SUPPORTS

- Force-tailored with the theater engineer command, an engineer brigade, or an engineer battalion to provide geospatial engineering.

### RULE OF ALLOCATION

- One per theater army.

Legend:
3-D – three-dimensional
IPB – intelligence preparation of the battlefield
JTF – joint task force
NGA – National Geospatial-Intelligence Agency
NSG – National System for Geospatial-Intelligence
TDA – tactical decision aid
TOE – table of organization and equipment

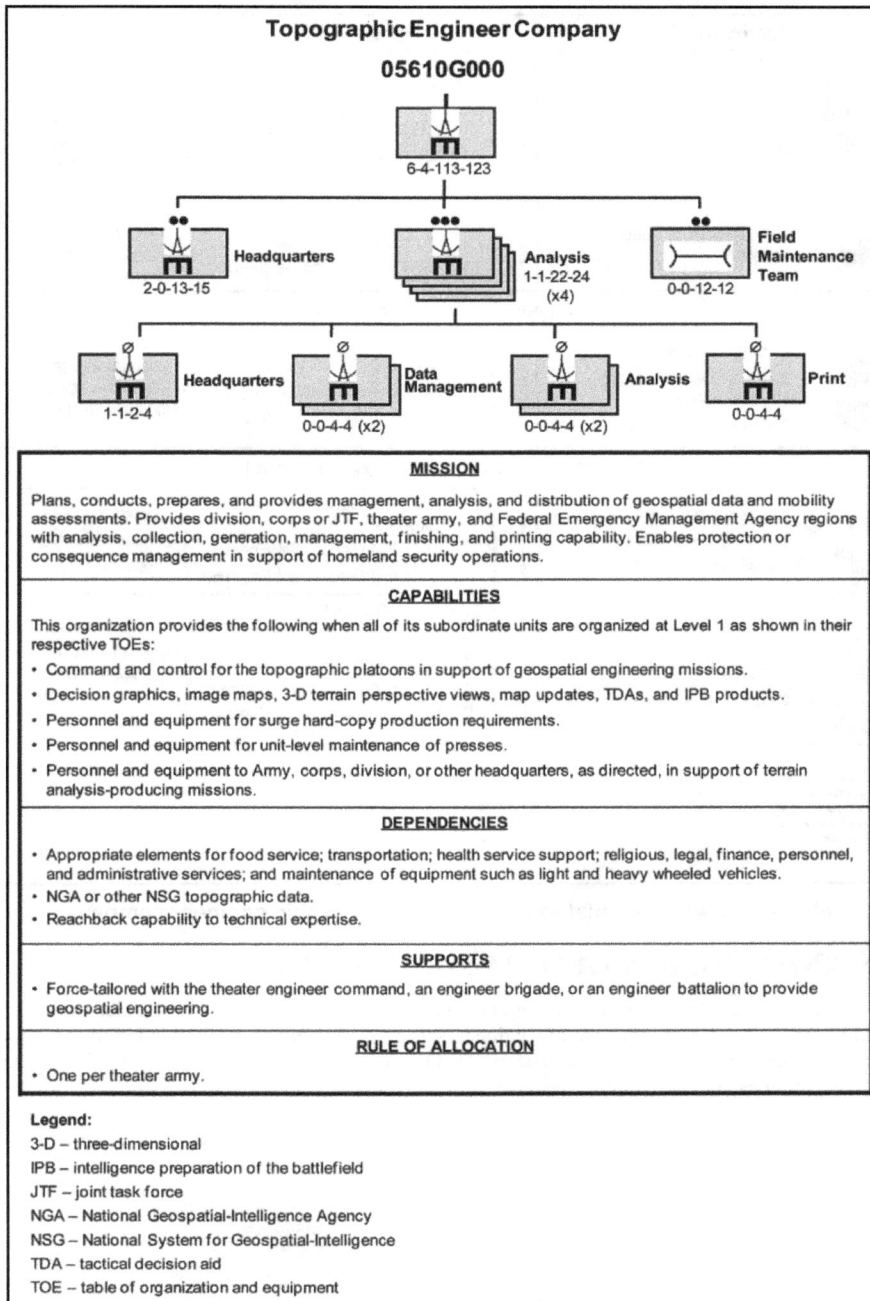

**Figure E-2. Topographic engineer company**

| Equipment | Personnel | Commo |
|---|---|---|
| **Headquarters, Analysis Platoon (1-1-2-4)** | | |
| 1 - T61494 Truck Utility HMMWV | 1 - 21B 0-2 Platoon Leader<br>1 - 12Y1 E-3 Vehicle Driver | C18378—FBCB2<br>N96248—DAGR<br>P49587—AN/VSQ-2<br>R68044—VRC-90F<br>Z00384—AN/PYQ-10 |
| 1 - T61494 Truck Utility HMMWV | 1 - 125D CW2 Geospatial Information Technician<br>1 - 12Y4 E-7 Platoon Sergeant | N96248—DAGR<br>P49587—AN/VSQ-2<br>R68044—VRC-90F<br>Z00384—AN/PYQ-10 |
| **Analysis Team, x2 (0-0-4-4)** | | |
| 1 - D10281 DTSS–L<br>1 - G42170 Generator Set 10 kilowatt 60 hertz<br>2 - T6149 Truck Utility HMMWV | 1 - 12Y3 E-6 Squad Leader<br>2 - 12Y1 E-4 Geospatial Engineer<br>1 - 12Y1 E-3 Geospatial Engineer | N96248—DAGR<br>R68044—VRC-90F<br>XXX852—IP Phone |
| **Data Management Team, x2 (0-0-4-4)** | | |
| 2 - D11498 DTSS–D<br>1 - T60081 Truck 4X4 LMTV<br>1 - T96564 Trailer LMTV | 1 - 12Y2 E-5 Geospatial Engineer Sergeant<br>1 - 12Y1 E-4 Geospatial Engineer<br>2 - 12Y1 E-3 Geospatial Engineer | XXX852—IP Phone<br>Z00384—AN/PYQ-10<br>Z99990—STE(2) |
| **Printing Team (0-0-4-4)** | | |
| 1 - T60081 Truck 4X4 LMTV<br>1 - Transit DTSS–HVMP | 1 - 12Y3 E-6 Squad Leader<br>1 - 12Y1 E-4 Geospatial Engineer<br>2 - 12Y1 E-3 Geospatial Engineer | N96248—DAGR<br>R68044—VRC-90F<br>XXX852—IP Phone<br>Z99990—STE(2) |

Legend:
DAGR – Defense Advanced GPS Receiver
DTSS–D – Digital Topographic Support System–Deployable
DTSS–HVMP – Digital Topographic Support System–High-Volume Map Production
DTSS–L – Digital Topographic Support System–Light
E-3 – private first class
E-4 – specialist/corporal
E-5 – sergeant
E-6 – staff sergeant
E-7 – sergeant first class
FBCB2 – Force XXI Battle Command, Brigade-and-Below
HMMWV – high-mobility multipurpose wheeled vehicle
IP – Internet protocol
LMTV – light medium tactical vehicle
CW2 – chief warrant officer 2

**Figure E-3. Analysis platoon within the topographic engineer company**

# CORPS AND DIVISION GEOSPATIAL ENGINEER TEAM

E-3.   The corps and division geospatial engineer team (see figure E-4) is led by a chief warrant officer 3 GI technician and a senior geospatial engineer sergeant. The team also includes an additional two geospatial engineer noncommissioned officers (NCOs) and five geospatial engineer Soldiers. The team's role and capabilities are discussed in chapter 2.

| Equipment | Personnel | Commo |
|---|---|---|
|  1 - T61494 Truck 4X4 HMMWV<br>1 - T95992 Trailer ¾ ton | ⚊ 1 - 125D CW3 Geospatial Information Technician | XXX852-IP Phone |
|  1 - T61630 M1113 HMMWV<br>1 - D10281 DTSS–L<br>1 - G42170 Generator Set<br>10 kilowatts 60 hertz | ⚊ 1 - 12Y4 E-7 Senior Geospatial Engineer Sergeant<br>⚊ 1 - 12Y2 E-5 Geospatial Engineer Sergeant<br>⚊ 1 - 12Y2 E-4 Geospatial Engineer<br>⚊ 1 - 12Y2 E-3 Geospatial Engineer | XXX852-IP Phone |
|  2 - D11408 DTSS–D | ⚊ 1 - 12Y2 E-5 Geospatial Engineer Sergeant<br>⚊⚊ 2 - 12Y2 E-4 Geospatial Engineer<br>⚊ 1 - 12Y2 E-3 Geospatial Engineer | |

Legend:
CW3 – chief warrant officer 3
DTSS–D – Digital Topographic Support System–Deployable
DTSS–L – Digital Topographic Support System–Light
E-3 – private first class
E-4 – specialist/corporal
E-5 – sergeant
E-7 – sergeant first class
HMMWV – high-mobility multipurpose wheeled vehicle
IP – Internet protocol

**Figure E-4. Corps/division geospatial engineer team**

## BRIGADE COMBAT TEAM GEOSPATIAL ENGINEER TEAM

E-4.    The BCT geospatial engineer team (see figure E-5) is led by a GI technician. The team also includes two geospatial NCOs and two geospatial engineers. The team's role and capabilities are discussed in chapter 2.

| Equipment | Personnel | Commo |
|---|---|---|
| 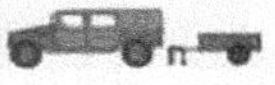 1 - T61494 Truck 4X4 HMMWV<br>1 - T95992 Trailer ¾ ton | ⚊ 1 - 12Y3/4 E-6/E-7 Squad Leader/NCOIC<br>⚊ 1 - 12Y1 E-3 Geospatial Engineer<br>⚊ 1 - 125D CW2 Geospatial Information Technician | R45543-VRC-92F<br>N96248-DAGR |
| 1 - T61630 M1113 HMMWV<br>1 - D10281 DTSS–L<br>1 - G42170 Generator Set 10 kilowatt 60 hertz | ⚊ 1 - 12Y2 E-5 Geospatial Engineer Sergeant<br>⚊ 1 - 12Y1 E-4 Geospatial Engineer | N96248-DAGR |

Legend:
BCT – brigade combat team
CW2 – chief warrant officer 2
DAGR – Defense Advanced GPS Receiver
DTSS–L – Digital Topographic Support SystemLight
E-3 – private first class
E-4 – specialist/corporal
E-5 – sergeant
E-6/E-7 – staff sergeant/sergeant first class
HMMWV – high-mobility multipurpose wheeled vehicle
NCOIC – noncommissioned officer in charge

**Figure E-5. BCT geospatial engineer team**

## BRIGADE GEOSPATIAL ENGINEER TEAM

E-5.    The geospatial engineer team in the modular support and functional brigades (figure E-6, page E-6) is led by a senior geospatial engineer sergeant. The team also includes another geospatial engineer sergeant and two geospatial engineers. The team's role and capabilities are discussed in chapter 2.

| Equipment | Personnel | Commo |
|---|---|---|
|  1 - T61494 Truck 4X4 HMMWV<br>1 - T95992 Trailer ¾ ton | 1 - 12Y3/4 E-6/E-7 Squad Leader/NCOIC<br>1 - 12Y1 E-3 Geospatial Engineer | R45543-VRC-92F<br>N96248-DAGR |
|  1 - T61630 M1113 HMMWV<br>1 - D10281 DTSS–L<br>1 - G42170 Generator Set 10 kilowatt 60 hertz | 1 - 12Y2 E-5 Geospatial Engineer Sergeant<br>1 - 12Y1 E-4 Geospatial Engineer | N96248-DAGR |

Legend:
DAGR – Defense Advanced GPS Receiver
DTSS–L – Digital Topographic Support SystemLight
E-3 – private first class
E-4 – specialist/corporal
E-5 – sergeant
E-6/E-7 – staff sergeant/sergeant first class
HMMWV – high-mobility multipurpose wheeled vehicle
NCOIC – noncommissioned officer in charge

Figure E-6. Brigade geospatial engineer team

## Appendix F

# Digital Topographic Support System

The DTSS is the geospatial engineering component of the ABCS that automates terrain analysis and visualization; database development, update, and management; and graphics reproduction in support of mission requirements. The DTSS provides the hardware and software necessary to develop and manage a geospatial database along with a software suite of GI processing capabilities that supports the Army with GI&S and special map reproduction. The DTSS is employed in various configurations at all echelons down to the BCT. This appendix describes the four DTSS configurations, which are DTSS–L, DTSS–D, DTSS–B, and DTSS–high volume map production (DTSS–HVMP).

## DIGITAL TOPOGRAPHIC SUPPORT SYSTEM–LIGHT

F-1. The DTSS–L (see figure F-1) is a completely self-contained system capable of storing and manipulating imagery, IMINT, and GI. It is housed in a lightweight multipurpose shelter that is mounted on a high-mobility multipurpose wheeled vehicle (HMMWV) and includes a tent extension to provide additional workspace. The DTSS–L can produce a variety of geospatial products (see appendix A) that can be exported in various formats for use in the ABCS that incorporate the commercial joint mapping tool kit and other GI&S programs such as Falcon View. In addition to creating tailored geospatial products, the DTSS–L provides access to the full capabilities of the image-processing and GI&S software packages.

Figure F-1. DTSS–L

## DIGITAL TOPOGRAPHIC SUPPORT SYSTEM–DEPLOYABLE

F-2. The DTSS–D (see figure F-2, page F-2) is a ruggedized computer system capable of receiving, formatting, creating, manipulating, merging, updating, storing, retrieving, and managing digital geospatial data and creating digital and hard-copy geospatial products. It is contained in hardened transit cases to facilitate deployment with tactical forces. It has similar capabilities to the DTSS–L except that it is not configured for vehicular mounting, which makes it well-suited for supporting light forces.

F-3. The DTSS–D is designed for a two-person geospatial engineer team. It includes a server and a storage device—created mostly from commercial off-the-shelf software—which are used to manage geospatial data. The DTSS–D comes equipped with the necessary communications capabilities to operate independently or in conjunction with a DTSS–L.

**Figure F-2. DTSS–D**

# DIGITAL TOPOGRAPHIC SUPPORT SYSTEM–BASE

F-4. The DTSS–B (see figure F-3) is a theater-level asset operated by the GPC from a fixed facility located with or near the ASCC headquarters. It gives geospatial engineers operating at theater the ability to generate and analyze geospatial data and augment existing databases to provide operational commanders with GI and geospatial products in support of mission requirements. The DTSS–B has increased data production capabilities over the other DTSS configurations, as well as enhanced feature and elevation data extraction tools. It also has increased data storage, management, and distribution/dissemination tools. The DTSS–B is also augmented with a direct link to commercial and national imagery.

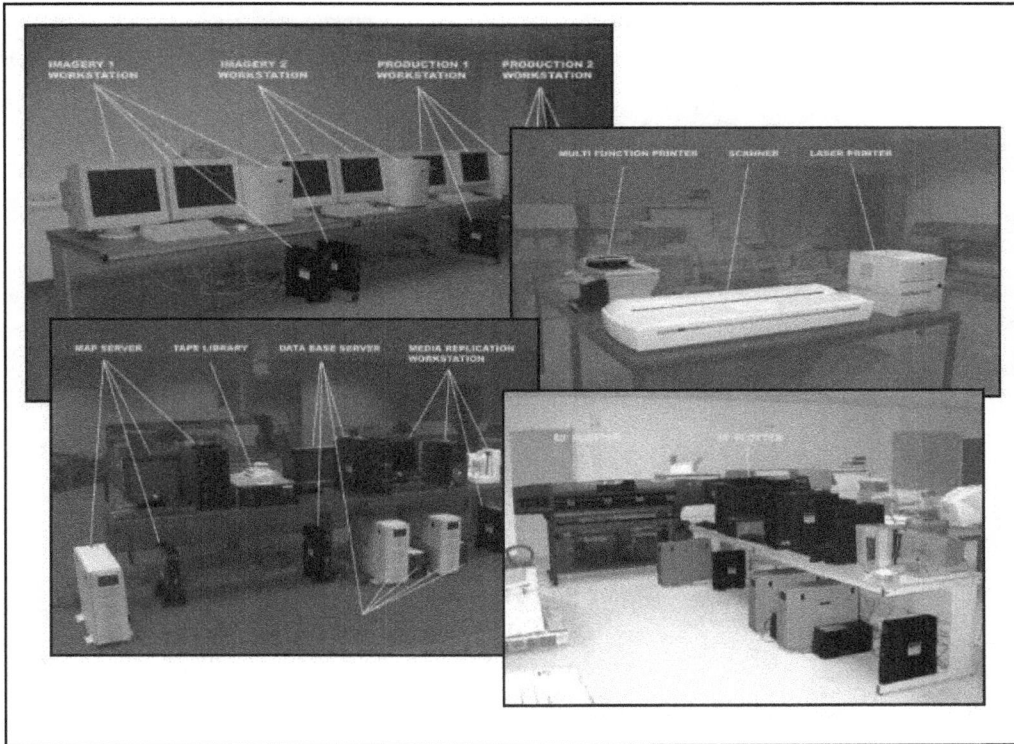

**Figure F-3. DTSS–B**

F-5. The DTSS–B is unique in that it is the only DTSS configuration with six analogous functions or functional slices, which are—

- Imagery slice to ingest and process national technical means imagery, extract 3-D features, generate and enhance DTED, process multispectral images, and support IPB.
- Production slice to produce TDAs, value-added data, map products, and 3-D visualization products.
- Database slice to store and manage data online with an automated archival capability.
- Map server slice to provide a Web-accessible digital database of products and data.
- Output slice to output hard-copy maps and limited reproduction of digital products.
- Media replication slice to replicate electronic storage media for dissemination.

# DIGITAL TOPOGRAPHIC SUPPORT SYSTEM–HIGH VOLUME MAP PRODUCTION

F-6. DTSS–HVMP (shown in figure F-4, page F-4) provides a tactical capability to rapidly reproduce large volumes of graphic material, including maps, charts, and situation overlays. It interfaces with other DTSS systems to receive and print their digital products. The DTSS–HVMP is capable of producing 2,500 full-color, large-format (22.5 inch by 29.5 inch), water-resistant copies per day. It has all of the software and hardware necessary to perform the same functions and capabilities of the DTSS–D, with the exception of hard-copy scanning. The DTSS–HVMP is configured to mount inside a 20-foot shelter on a standard Army 5-ton truck.

**Figure F-4. DTSS–HVMP**

# Glossary

The glossary lists acronyms/abbreviations and terms with Army or joint definitions, and other selected terms. Where Army and joint definitions are different, (Army) follows the term. Terms or acronyms for which ATTP 3-34.80 is the proponent manual (the authority) are marked with an asterisk (*).

## SECTION I–ACRONYMS AND ABBREVIATIONS

| Acronym/Term | Definition |
|---|---|
| 2-D | two-dimensional |
| 3-D | three-dimensional |
| AA | avenue of approach |
| ABCS | Army Battle Command System |
| ACR | armored cavalry regiment |
| AGC | Army Geospatial Center |
| AO | area of operations |
| AOR | area of responsibility |
| ASCC | Army Service component command |
| ATTN | attention |
| ATTP | Army tactics, techniques, and procedures |
| BCT | brigade combat team |
| BDA | battle damage assessment |
| C2 | command and control |
| CADRG | compressed arc digitized raster graphic |
| CCIR | commander's critical information requirement |
| CCM | cross-country mobility |
| CD | compact disc |
| CIB | Controlled Image Base |
| COA | course of action |
| COO | combined obstacle overlay |
| COP | common operational picture |
| CP | command post |
| CRM | composite risk management |
| D3A | decide, detect, deliver, and assess |
| DA | Department of the Army |
| DBMS | database management system |
| DCGS | Distributed Common Ground System |
| DCGS–A | distributed common ground system–Army |
| DEM | digital elevation model |
| DLA | Defense Logistics Agency |
| DOD | Department of Defense |
| DTED | Digital Terrain Elevation Data |

| Acronym/Term | Definition |
|---|---|
| DTSS | digital topographic support system |
| DTSS–B | digital topographic support system–base |
| DTSS–D | digital topographic support system–deployable |
| DTSS–L | digital topographic support system–light |
| DTSS–HVMP | digital topographic support system–high volume map production |
| EA | engagement area |
| ENCOORD | engineer coordinator |
| FM | field manual |
| G-2 | assistant chief of staff, intelligence |
| G-3 | assistant chief of staff, operations |
| G-4 | assistant chief of staff, logistics |
| G-5 | assistant chief of staff, plans |
| GCC | geographic combatant commander |
| GEOINT | geospatial intelligence |
| GeoPDF | geospatial portable document format |
| GI | geospatial information |
| GI&S | geospatial intelligence and services |
| GPC | geospatial planning cell |
| HMMWV | high-mobility multipurpose wheeled vehicle |
| HN | host nation |
| HPT | high-payoff target |
| HPTL | high-payoff target list |
| HUMINT | human intelligence |
| HVT | high-value target |
| IMINT | imagery intelligence |
| IPB | intelligence preparation of the battlefield |
| IR | information requirement |
| ISR | intelligence, surveillance, and reconnaissance |
| ITD | interim terrain data |
| JOG–A | joint operational graphic–air |
| JP | joint publication |
| JTF | joint task force |
| KM | knowledge management |
| LIDAR | light detection and ranging |
| LOC | lines of communication |
| LOS | line of sight |
| MANSCEN | Maneuver Support Center |
| MCOO | modified combined obstacle overlay |
| MDMP | military decisionmaking process |
| METT-TC | mission, enemy, terrain and weather, troops and support available, time |

| Acronym/Term | Definition |
|---|---|
| | available, civil considerations |
| MI | military intelligence |
| MLC | military load class |
| NASIC | National Air and Space Intelligence Center |
| NCO | noncommissioned officer |
| NCOIC | noncommissioned officer in charge |
| NGA | National Geospatial-Intelligence Agency |
| NGIC | National Ground Intelligence Center |
| NIPRNET | Non-Secure Internet Protocol Router Network |
| NSG | National System for Geospatial-Intelligence |
| NST | National Geospatial-Intelligence Agency support team |
| OAKOC | observation and fields of fire, avenues of approach, key and decisive terrain, obstacles, cover and concealment |
| OE | operational environment |
| OIC | officer in charge |
| PMESII-PT | political, military, economic, social, information, infrastructure, physical environment, time |
| RFI | request for information |
| RI | relevant information |
| S-2 | intelligence staff officer |
| S-3 | operations staff officer |
| S-4 | logistics staff officer |
| S-5 | plans staff officer |
| SIGINT | signals intelligence |
| SIPRNET | SECRET Internet Protocol Router Network |
| SOP | standing operating procedure |
| TC | training circular |
| TDA | tactical decision aid |
| TGD | theater geospatial database |
| TLM | topographic line map |
| TRADOC | United States Army Training and Doctrine Command |
| USACE | United States Army Corps of Engineers |
| USAES | United States Army Engineer School |
| UTP | Urban Tactical Planner |
| VITD | vector interim terrain data |
| VMAP | vector map |

## SECTION II–TERMS

**\*complex terrain**

(Army) A geographical area consisting of an urban center larger than a village and/or of two or more types of restrictive terrain or environmental conditions occupying the same space. Restrictive terrain or environmental conditions include, but are not limited to, slope, high altitude, forestation, severe weather, and urbanization.

**\*geospatial information**

(Army) The foundation information upon which all other information about the physical environment is referenced to form the common operational picture.

**\*terrain analysis**

(Army) The study of the terrain's properties and how they change over time, with use, and under varying weather conditions. Terrain analysis starts with the collection, verification, processing, revision, and construction of source data. It requires the analysis of climatology (current and forecasted weather conditions), natural and man-made features, and enemy or friendly vehicle performance metrics. Terrain analysis is a technical process and requires the expertise of geospatial information technicians and geospatial engineers.

# References

## SOURCES USED

The following sources are either quoted or paraphrased in this publication.

### ARMY PUBLICATIONS

FM 1-02. *Operational Terms and Graphics* {MCRP 5-12A}. 21 September 2004.

FM 2-0. *Intelligence*. 17 May 2004.

FM 2-01.3. *Intelligence Preparation of the Battlefield/Battlespace {MCRP 2-3A}*. 15 October 2009.

FM 3-0. *Operations*. 27 February 2008.

FM 3-06. *Urban Operations*. 26 October 2006.

FM 3-20.96. *Cavalry Squadron*. 12 March 2010.

FM 3-25.26. *Map Reading and Land Navigation*. 18 January 2005.

FM 3-34. *Engineer Operations*. 2 April 2009.

FM 3-34.22. *Engineer Operations–Brigade Combat Team and Below*. 11 February 2009.

FM 3-34.170. *Engineer Reconnaissance {MCWP 3-17.4}*. 25 March 2008.

FM 3-90.5. *The Combined Arms Battalion*. 7 April 2008.

FM 3-90.6. *The Brigade Combat Team*. 4 August 2006.

FM 3-90.12. *Combined Arms Gap-Crossing Operations {MCWP 3-17.1}*. 1 July 2008.

FM 5-0. *The Operations Process*. 26 March 2010.

FM 5-19. *Composite Risk Management*. 21 August 2006.

FM 5-410. *Military Soils Engineering*. 23 December 1992.

FM 5-480. *Port Construction and Repair*. 12 December 1990.

FM 5-484. *Multiservice Procedures for Well-Drilling Operations {NAVFACP-1065; AFMAN 32-1072}*. 8 March 1994.

FM 6-0. *Mission Command: Command and Control of Army Forces*. 11 August 2003.

FM 6-01.1. *Knowledge Management Section*. 29 August 2008.

FM 6-20-10. *Tactics, Techniques, and Procedures for the Targeting Process {MCRP 3-1.6.14}*. 8 May 1996.

FM 7-15. *The Army Universal Task List*. 27 February 2009.

FM 55-50. *Army Water Transport Operations*. 30 September 1993.

FM 90-7. *Combined Arms Obstacle Integration*. 29 September 1994.

FMI 2-01. *Intelligence, Surveillance, and Reconnaissance (ISR) Synchronization*. 11 November 2008.

### JOINT PUBLICATIONS

JP 2-03. *Geospatial Intelligence Support to Joint Operations*. 22 March 2007.

JP 3-33. *Joint Task Force Headquarters*. 16 February 2007.

JP 3-34. *Joint Engineer Operations*. 12 February 2007.

JP 5-0. *Joint Operation Planning*. 26 December 2006.

## DOCUMENTS NEEDED

These documents must be available to the intended users of this publication. DA forms are available on the APD website (www.apd.army.mil).

DA Form 2028. *Recommended Changes to Publications and Blank Forms*.

# READINGS RECOMMENDED

These readings contain relevant supplemental information.

NSG Publication 1-0. *Geospatial Intelligence (GEOINT) Basic Doctrine*. September 2006. (http://www.fas.org/irp/agency/nga/doctrine.pdf)

# Index

This page intentionally left blank.

ATTP 3-34.80 (FM 3-34.230, FM 5-33, and TC 5-230)
29 July 2010

By order of the Secretary of the Army:

**GEORGE W. CASEY, JR.**
*General, United States Army*
*Chief of Staff*

Official:

**JOYCE E. MORROW**
*Administrative Assistant to the*
*Secretary of the Army*
*1018201*

**DISTRIBUTION:**

*Active Army, Army National Guard, and United States Army Reserve*: To be distributed according to the initial distribution number 110451 requirements for ATTP 3-34.80.

www.ingramcontent.com/pod-product-compliance
Lightning Source LLC
Chambersburg PA
CBHW080207300326
41934CB00038B/3399